TRAINS of Discovery

An observation car of the Yosemite Valley Railroad, ca. 1908, when passenger trains, like women's hats, were in fashion. Courtesy of the Yosemite National Park Research Library.

TRAINS of Discovery

WESTERN RAILROADS AND THE NATIONAL PARKS

Fourth Edition, Revised

ALFRED RUNTE

ROBERTS RINEHART PUBLISHERS

Boulder, Colorado

DEDICATION

Still to good friends, and good trains, and all the wonderful memories we share of both. And especially to my friends who have helped me tell this story—Walter Smith, Al Richmond, J. Craig Thorpe, Carlos Schwantes, Richard J. Orsi, Carsten Lien, Lisa Mighetto, Bill Johnson, Joseph Vranich, Michael Frome, Marcy Culpin, Carl Bajema, David Corbin, Arthur Lloyd, Frank Potter, Dan Monaghan, Gordon Chappell, Bruce Heard, Robin W. Winks, and Richard M. Bressler.

And with special thanks to Max and Thelma Biegert, who still dare to dream of bigger and better things.

COVER: Original railroad poster, *Absaroka Mountains, Montana, Northern Pacific Railway*, by Gustav Krollmann, circa 1931. Spring in the Paradise Valley envelopes the slopes of Emigrant Peak, regally positioned to frame a passenger train southbound for Gardiner Gateway and Yellowstone National Park. Poster size 40 by 30 inches. Author's Collection.

HALF TITLE VIGNETTE: "'North Coast Limited' at Livingston, Montana," original photo-illustration of the Northern Pacific Railroad's premier passenger train, from *Wonderland*, 1904. Courtesy of the Pacific Northwest Collection, University of Washington Libraries, Seattle.

Contents

"All aboard on the *Empire Builder*...," photograph from *Glacier Park in Pictures*, a Great Northern Railway brochure, ca. 1940. Courtesy of the Pacific Northwest Collection, University of Washington Libraries, Seattle.

Preface to the Fourth Edition

The progress of *Trains of Discovery* through four separate editions reflects the popularity of a unique and colorful relationship, that binding the fortunes of America's railroads to the future of the national parks. Indeed, as these pages have noted over the years, the story is far more complex than the familiar tale of preservation versus commerce. As often, railroad officials and early environmentalists were working for the same goal—a landscape mirroring the best of the American imagination. Beauty, like any other commodity, could be sold to an eager public. The secret was building and promoting railroads always with an eye to the joys of pleasure travel.

The Northern Pacific Railroad headlined its *North Coast Limited* as the "Companion of Mountains," for example. Nor did such phraseology promote the grandeur of the West purely as a matter of expedience. Railroad executives, as much as anyone, also lamented that the region's conquest and settlement marked the end of the American wilderness.

In that spirit of retrospection, I intended the first and second editions of *Trains of Discovery* for historians, national park visitors, and the general public. Each audience, I hoped, would act in synergy with the others, reaffirming the need to save some of the great trains and national landscapes of the past. Yet a third edition of the book, published in 1994, included more outstanding examples of railroad promotional art. Any historian could spend years, I noted, merely searching out the artistic contributions of a single railroad company.

This 1904 *Wonderland* photo-illustration depicts from top to bottom: "Northern Pacific Railway Observation Car . . . Day Coach . . . Dining Car . . . Standard Pullman Sleeping Car." Courtesy of the Pacific Northwest Collection, University of Washington Libraries, Seattle.

I have added new illustrations here, both contemporary and historical. Similarly, I have rewritten Chapters Four and Six to reflect recent developments bearing on the history of the Yosemite Valley and Grand Canyon railways. Unique to this edition is Chapter Seven, containing practical information for the traveler about the best of the surviving trains themselves. Where is it still possible to rediscover the national parks using railroad transportation? How do I get there, in other words, and what should I be looking for when I do?

In retrospect, it is amazing that travel by train in the United States continues to flourish anywhere. One by one, America's railroads came to believe that carrying passengers simply did not pay. At least, freight traffic paid considerably more, and never complained about delays, missed connections, or the lack of speed and service. Besides, Americans were falling in love with their cars, rejecting train schedules and crowded terminals for the asserted freedom of the open road.

Even as Amtrak began operations in May 1971, many analysts believed it symbolized only the beginning of the end for all but passenger trains linking densely populated urban corridors. It was then, in painful recognition of the heritage and opportunities the nation stood to lose, that I began writing the series of articles that would lead to this book. Not only did I lament the declining fortunes of the passenger train as a form of transportation, more, I longed for that sense of national accomplishment it had so profoundly come to represent.

However selfishly or unintentionally, the railroads had fostered genuine feelings of regional pride and cultural identity. Trains themselves were commonly named for national landmarks or in celebration of bold ideas. Color schemes and interiors reflected the history and uniqueness of the passing countryside. In contrast, the interstate highways that paralleled the railroads beginning in the 1960s seemed barren of identity. Built for speed, superhighways either defaced or bypassed the best regional scenery, and, succumbing to billboards and fast food outlets, generally featured the same examples of cultural monotony their motorists had left behind.

Would the West, like the East, resign itself to conformity, turning from promotion as art to advertising as litter? Would its highways similarly be choked with billboards and its mountains smothered with condominiums? Would Amtrak also turn its back on the greatness of its heritage, choosing the fast track to "Finger-Lickin' Junction" in the pursuit of so-called market share? Or would the West fight to maintain its uniqueness, eschewing the golden arches and insisting, instead, on another *real* golden age? Above all, why had railroad executives historically embraced, then forsaken, a genuine commitment to the traveling public through the promotion of beautiful trains and beautiful landscapes?

As further incentive to continue my search for answers, I was privileged in 1980 to begin four seasons as a ranger naturalist in Yosemite National Park. I owe a great deal to my friends and colleagues in the National Park Service, who supported my preparation of a series of evening programs on the history, meaning, and management of the national parks, including the contributions of the western railroads. In 1989, that history was reaffirmed in the reinaugural of the Grand Canyon Railway. Later, in 1994, then a trustee of the National Parks and Conservation Association, I helped promote its seventy-fifth anniversary around a transcontinental trip by rail, obtaining permission for our special train to enter Grand Canyon National Park over the Santa Fe and Grand Canyon railways. The *American Orient Express* soon followed elegantly in our footsteps, recreating an era that many believed had forever vanished with the demise of luxury rail passenger service.

Inevitably, such events have motivated my continuing reevaluation of the subject of this book. Delightfully, what began as a look into history now recounts the many visionaries who once again are looking forward, confident that rail passenger service will be every bit as important to our future. That remains my conviction, too. The preservation of our national parks and wilderness ultimately requires eliminating the deluge of motor vehicles. Then, too, conservation is not just a matter of preserving parks and wilderness; it further demands our refusing to take for granted the naturalness enveloping our daily lives. No less committed to that larger ideal—saving all that is beautiful in the American landscape—I take pleasure in welcoming readers aboard this fourth departing section of *Trains of Discovery*.

Introduction

The United States, recognized for its Declaration of Independence and the Constitution, has also bequeathed to the world its most copied example of landscape democracy—the national park idea. Historically, credit for the American invention of national parks has gone to John Muir, members of the Sierra Club, and other like-minded idealists. But there is another side to the story. The more historians have examined the social, cultural, and intellectual origins of the national park system, the more they have discovered the great debt owed to the railroads of the American West for both the existence and promotion of all the original park areas. Granted, that support was profit motivated. Nevertheless, without the assistance of the railroads, it is fair to argue that Yellowstone, Yosemite, Glacier, and the Grand Canyon, among other national parks, might never have been established in the first place.

Regrettably, one of the first casualties of America's love affair with the automobile was that original "pragmatic alliance," which at its height, celebrated the protection rather than consumption of the American land. In time, as the majority of travelers retreated to the privacy of their own cars, the railroads themselves saw no need to maintain their former sense of identity with the environment. Railroading became strictly a business, rather than an investment in constructive social change. The deeper the automobile cut into the profits of passenger railroading, for example, the more the railroads reaffirmed their primary interest in freight, and then in freight traffic only.

Railroad Access Routes to the Western National Parks

Railroad Lines

① Great Northern, Union Pacific, Northern Pacific railroads

② Great Northern Railway, mainline connections to Glacier National Park

③ Yellowstone Branch, Union Pacific Railroad

④ Yellowstone Branch, Northern Pacific Railroad

⑤ Cody Branch (Yellowstone gateway); Chicago, Burlington & Quincy Railroad

⑥ Cedar City Branch (Zion, Bryce, Northern Rim Grand Canyon gateway), Union Pacific Railroad

⑦ Grand Canyon Branch; Atchison, Topeka & Santa Fe Railway

⑧ Yosemite Valley Railroad

⑨ Southern Pacific Railroad

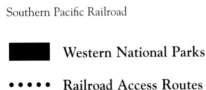

Western National Parks

••••• Railroad Access Routes

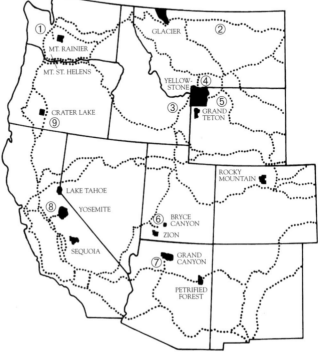

The platform of the El Portal Station, gateway to Yosemite, at train time, ca. 1916. Passengers arriving on the Yosemite Valley Railroad board waiting motor stages for the remaining one hour and thirty-five minute trip to Yosemite Valley. Courtesy of the Yosemite National Park Research Library.

Suddenly, people were an inconvenience, or worse, a drag on the entire system. Losing sight of their own history, railroad executives for-got the importance of passenger railroading as a means of courting influential friends and allies. Meanwhile, the very highways that had carried off those now "burdensome" passengers were also paving the way for trucks, in other words, for the railroads' worst competitive nightmare. Granted, the automobile was a technology whose time had arrived. Granted, too, government regulation was generally no friend of the railroads. Yet, by declaring that every passenger had to go, the railroads lost public confidence. The positive business climate that lay behind their support of the national parks gradually soured, then evap-orated altogether. Transportation in the United States became an "all or nothing" proposition. The automobile was "in"; the passenger train was "out." Critics who dared list the car's shortcomings—from tens of thousands of annual deaths to its drain on land and finite resources— still had nowhere left to turn. Rather, in the face of what appeared to

be the ultimate demise of America's railroad system, to many there
seemed to be no other choice than to embrace automobile culture.

Undoubtedly, historians will continue debating endlessly which cau-
sation came first, the proverbial chicken (public abandonment of the
railroads) or the egg (the railroads' abandonment of the public). A reasonable interpretation would hold that both evolved simultaneously,
feeding one upon the other in a descending spiral of negative reinforce-
ment. In either case, one result was the erosion of the railroads' historical commitment to fostering an American sense of place. Especially for
the national parks, the transition from public transportation to automobiles cost the parks a critical social "filter," a fair yet effective means of
asking every visitor to think first of the *privilege* of access.

True, public transportation is more restrictive, but that again is just
the point. The national parks were intended to be the antithesis of civilization, the natural antidote to our daily diet of me-first commercial-
ism. Historically, public transportation had encouraged all park visitors
to ask themselves this question: Is the privilege of my being here recreation enough? Does this park, free of all distractions, inspire me in and
of itself?

Thanks to the automobile, it became all too easy for any visitor to
dodge that responsibility, to confuse the privilege of entering the parks
as license to alter them. Access meant not only the "right" to see the
parks and their wonders, but also to insist, in the process, that the Park
Service accommodate everyone's fad or obsession, be it mobile homes,
bars, ski lifts, or snowmobiles. Gone was the need to make choices,
whether, to cite another example, it was more important to bring along
the family stereo or another change of clothes. As the use of automobiles proliferated, so did the public's taste for distractive or even
destructive pursuits.

In retrospect, the decline of America's railroads had had repercus-
sions far beyond suburbia, where former centers of community
identity—the courthouse, town square, or downtown railroad station—had also been bypassed and forgotten. Lost to the parks as well
was that sense of community and shared responsibility that railroad
travel had fostered, not to mention its supporting *images* of responsibility—the glowing package of literature, photographs, and commissioned works of art whose constant, subliminal message had been one
of public stewardship.

Finally, there is renewed hope that history will repeat itself, that the trend of the 1990s is back to public transportation. Indeed, some of the most encouraging signs are once again to be found at popular entrances to the national parks. On September 17, 1989, for example, the first passenger train in twenty-one years left Williams, Arizona, for Grand Canyon National Park over the fully restored Grand Canyon Railway. Similarly, since the mid-1980s, upward of 300,000 people annually have been recapturing a sense of the past at Denali (Mount McKinley) National Park in Alaska. Three major carriers—the Alaska Railroad, Holland America Westours, and Princess Tours—have combined to provide the latest in rail travel amenities, including full-length vista domes and modern sightseeing coaches. At Denali, wilderness enthusiasts may rediscover what the national parks were like a century ago, when all of them were far removed from the boundaries of civilization.

Glacier National Park, in northwestern Montana, is also still renowned for its rustic sense of isolation. On the main line of Amtrak's *Empire Builder*, Glacier further holds the distinction of being the one national park in the continental United States that never lost its rail passenger service. Consequently, Glacier, like Denali, has long preserved a glimpse of that golden age of passenger railroading in the West, during which not only Glacier but also Yellowstone, Yosemite, Mount Rainier, and the Grand Canyon were directly accessible via passenger trains.

With daily service to Denali, Glacier, and the Grand Canyon already available—and with more restorations in the offing—Americans have another once-in-a-lifetime opportunity to honestly reassess the priorities and principles of their national parks. Public transportation, to reemphasize, is a responsible social filter, allowing young and old, weak and strong, the privilege of access. What it filters out is lack of commitment, that all-too-common tendency to take the parks for granted simply because the automobile makes them easy to reach. A family planning a trip to Europe would never dream of packing everything it owns, nor of insisting, on arrival, that Europe make every shrine fully accessible to cars, buses, and mobile homes. Yet, many Americans demand that the national parks provide that very level of access—access serving the vehicle they happen to own rather than the uniqueness of the place they allegedly hope to enjoy.

More reliance on trains, and less on automobiles, could restore our ability to visit the national parks without destroying them in the process, again teaching us how to provide for everyone who wants to see these special areas without resorting to the very facilities, activities, and levels of congestion that undermine the integrity of the natural environment. Inside the national parks, more trams, shuttle buses, and other so-called people movers—such as those currently in use at Yosemite and Grand Canyon—could ferry visitors between trains and the most popular points of interest.

And so again, in the spirit of those earlier editions of *Trains of Discovery*, in the spirit of commitment to what is *best* for our national parks, I invite everyone to reconsider the possibilities of redesigning all of our major parks entirely around public transportation. Heed again that familiar command, "All aboard!", that now reechoes in the shadow of Mount McKinley and El Tovar. Join me as our streamliner of history, further propelled by the stunning artistry of railroad promotion, glides westward toward America's wonderlands—the national parks.

The Alaska Railroad is one of the three major companies providing distinctive rail excursions to Denali (Mount McKinley) National Park via Anchorage and Fairbanks. Shown here are the cars of the Alaska Railroad and the full-length luxury domes of the *McKinley Explorer*, operated by Holland America Line—Westours. Courtesy of Holland America Line—Westours.

All of the elements of popularizing the West as America's romantic terminus are present in Thomas Moran's great painting, *The Grand Canyon of the Yellowstone* (1872). Courtesy of the National Museum of American Art, Smithsonian Institution. Lent by U.S. Department of the Interior, National Park Service.

Left. This evocative painting of Mount St. Helens graced the Northern Pacific Railroad's 1931 guidebook *The Northern Pacific Coast Vacation Land*. Author's collection. *Right.* In this elegant bas-relief sculpture from *Wonderland*, 1903, two artistic cupids unveil their own rendition of the Grand Canyon of the Yellowstone. Courtesy of the Pacific Northwest Collection, University of Washington Libraries, Seattle.

ONE

The Romantic Terminus

The western margin of this continent is built of a succession of mountain chains folded in broad corrugations, like waves of stone upon whose seaward base beat the mild small breakers of the Pacific. By far the grandest of these ranges is the Sierra Nevada, . . . its crest a line of sharp, snowy peaks springing into the sky and catching the alpenglow *long after the sun has set for all the rest of America.*

Clarence King, 1871

Anyone who has thumbed through the pages of an old newspaper or magazine, or gazed intently into the faded reality of a long-forgotten photograph, may recall the sensation of being "lost," if only momentarily, in the era depicted. What follows is a similar attempt to recapture the spirit of a particular age in all its visual drama and literary exuberance. The subject is railroads—their destination, the national parks. Singled out for emphasis is the eighty-year period between 1880 and 1960, during which Americans were either dependent on rail transportation or still accustomed to considering passenger trains as a serious option for pleasure travel. In this volume, the reader will find original pieces of railroad art or advertising copy, carefully reproduced to reflect the elegance of their initial unveiling. Similarly, the photographs have been chosen to suggest the excitement of visiting the national parks during that age when the word "West" was still synonymous with high adventure

Well into the twentieth century, as the artistic and literary achievements of the Romantic Movement were still fresh in the minds of Americans, the railroads of the West enjoyed a marketing advantage that was second to none. Theirs was the "romantic terminus." Americans have been drawn to the West not only by its history but also by its topography. Westward expansion provided Americans with the opportunity to play out their final act of territorial development against such imposing backdrops as Yellowstone, Mount Rainier, the Grand Canyon, and the Yosemite Valley. These very western

The breathtaking scenery along the main line of the Great Northern Railway lent an added dimension to the comings and goings of the company's classic trains. Courtesy of Richard Piper.

landscapes inspired the first national parks: ecology was not the nation's concern at the turn of the century, but rather, the preservation of these last vestiges of the unspoiled "romantic horizon" was at stake.

Among all the publicists of the region, the railroads were without rivals in their ability to bring the West into the living rooms of the American people with special attention given to its cultural and topographical significance. The development of the national parks coincided perfectly with the lines' marketing strategy. Economically speaking, the enticement of settlers and city-builders from the security of the East to the uncertainties of the new frontier demanded the stimulation that only the power of suggestion could provide. Standard advertising copy wrapped the West in an array of superlatives, giving special attention to its unlimited potential for economic growth, built on a vast foundation of natural resources. Underground minerals and fields not yet broken to the plow were hard to visualize, however; potential was not reality. In the meantime, people needed some tangible evidence of abundance. Thus, by creatively drawing attention to the scale of western topography, the railroads discovered one subtle means of suggesting to prospective migrants that, as claimed, the region must indeed be equally well-endowed with hidden wealth.

Rail travel was, in this respect, a means to a greater end; those who were tourists one day might in fact decide to become settlers the next. In another sense, tourism was also a lucrative end in itself. For decades, Americans in search of spectacular scenery had traveled almost exclusively to such eastern wonders as the Natural Bridge in Virginia, the Hudson River highlands, and Niagara Falls in New York. With the completion of the first transcontinental railroad in 1869, these wealthy patrons of America's great eastern resorts could realistically think about seeing the West as well.

For the next half century, the railroads of the region did everything possible to stimulate that interest. Partly a quest for profits, partly a means of achieving greater recognition and prestige, the campaign elevated railroad executives to positions of importance and influence as patrons of the arts. As early as 1903, for example, the Santa Fe Railway began acquiring paintings about the Grand Canyon, the Petrified Forest, and other southwestern subjects for its stations and executive suites. Similarly, in 1898 the Southern Pacific Railroad founded *Sunset*, a monthly magazine supporting scores of creative individuals, especially artists, photographers, and journalists.

Whatever the medium or the occasion, national parks were primary attractions for promotional efforts. As masterpieces of nature, the parks set the standard for artworks that the railroads hoped would attract both settlers and tourists to the romantic West. Today, awareness of ecological needs has diffused much of that initial innocence, spontaneity, and enthusiasm for national park promotion. Nevertheless, the color and elegance of the period are timeless.

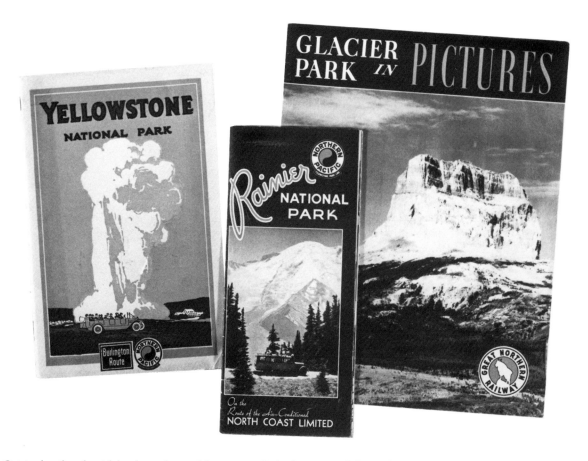

Original railroad guidebooks and pamphlet covers. *Left:* Courtesy of the author. *Center and right:* Courtesy of the Pacific Northwest Collection, University of Washington Libraries, Seattle.

TWO ⊗
THE NORTHERN PACIFIC RAILROAD
Yellowstone Park Line

The traveler who has journeyed eastward to climb the castled crags of Rhineland and survey the mighty peaks and wondrous glaciers of the Alps, who has . . . gazed upon the marvelous creations of Michelangelo and Da Vinci; and stood within the shadow of the pyramids,—may well turn westward to view the greater wonders of his own land.

Beyond the Great Lakes, far from the hum of New England factories, far from the busy throngs of Broadway, from the smoke and grime of iron cities, and the dull, prosaic life of many another Eastern town, lies a region which may justly be designated the Wonderland of the World.

Charles S. Fee, General Passenger Agent, Northern Pacific Railroad, 1885

Among the methods of conservation in the United States, the national park idea has been heralded as America's purest expression of landscape democracy. As a result, the mere suggestion that an institution so famous for its idealism and philanthropy would receive a crucial boost from industry may seem almost sacrilegious. According to popular tradition, the explorers who opened Yellowstone in 1870 conceived the national park idea while unraveling the mysteries of the region. But at best, ecology and altruism were afterthoughts of the Yellowstone Park campaign. From the outset, establishment of the park owed far more to the financier Jay Cooke and to officials of the Northern Pacific Railroad—all of whom, upon completion of the line, expected to profit from the territory as a great tourist resort.

As the more patriotic and unselfish account, the popular depiction of the origins of Yellowstone National Park has obviously been less difficult to embrace. According to this version, the national park idea was not born in a corporate boardroom; instead, it came into being on the night of September 19, 1870, when members of the celebrated Washburn Expedition settled down around their campfire to share

13

Standing fifty feet high, with a thirty-foot arch, the entrance to Yellowstone National Park, at Gardiner, Montana, welcomed visitors arriving via the Northern Pacific Railroad. From *Wonderland*, 1904, courtesy of the Pacific Northwest Collection, University of Washington Libraries, Seattle.

impressions of the wonderland that they had just finished exploring. Apparently, one of the men proposed that each member of the party claim a tract of land surrounding the canyon or the geyser basins for personal gain. Cornelius Hedges, a young lawyer from Helena, Montana, strongly disagreed, and pleaded with the explorers to abandon any private ambitions in the interest of promoting Yellowstone as a great national park for all Americans to own and enjoy. Nathaniel Pitt Langford, the noted publicist of the expedition, recorded the following in his diary: "His suggestions met with an instantaneous and favorable response from all—except one—of the members of our party, and each hour since the matter was first broached, our enthusiasm has increased." Thus, Langford concluded his entry for September 20, "I lay awake half of last night thinking about it; and if my wakefulness deprived my bed-fellow (Hedges) of any sleep, he has only himself and his disturbing National Park proposition to answer for it."

No less than Yellowstone's natural wonders, park bears have fascinated visitors since the turn of the century. Photo-illustration from *Wonderland*, 1904, courtesy of the Pacific Northwest Collection, University of Washington Libraries, Seattle.

There is only one nagging doubt about the accuracy of this state-ment: Langford did not publish these words until 1905, fully thirty-five years after the event. By then, of course, he and his colleagues had had numerous opportunities to amend their accounts of the expedition in light of the growing fame of the national park idea. Certainly there is something suspicious in the fact that, despite their reported enthusi-asm, not one of the eighteen men present around that Yellowstone campfire ever mentioned the national park idea in the articles and speeches prepared immediately afterward. In either case, even if Langford's account were credible, some very important names would still be missing from his story, most notably Jay Cooke, promoter and financier of the Northern Pacific Railroad extension project, and Cooke's office manager, A. B. Nettleton.

Indeed, the explorers' discussion around their campfire that mid-September evening could not have taken place in ignorance of the plans of the Northern Pacific Railroad. Langford must have informed all of the men about Jay Cooke's intentions, including Henry D. Washburn, the surveyor general of Montana and nominal leader of the expedition. Three months prior to the venture, Langford had met per-sonally with Cooke at the latter's estate just outside Philadelphia. Not only did Cooke retain Langford to promote Yellowstone as part of a publicity campaign to secure funding for the railroad, he probably sug-gested the Washburn Expedition itself. By then, Cooke realized that his right-of-way through south-central Montana would bring him within forty or fifty miles of Yellowstone. Obviously, with such a great wonderland lying along his main line to the Pacific, Cooke stood to become the direct beneficiary of any publicity aimed at introducing the region to prospective travelers.

Meanwhile, following the expedition of 1870, Nathaniel Langford returned east to lecture in New York, Philadelphia, and Washington, D.C., on behalf of the Northern Pacific. Here again, his writings and statements reveal that he acted more as a promoter rather than as a concerned private citizen speaking only for the protection of Yellowstone. At every opportunity, Langford trumpeted the building of the Northern Pacific Railroad, specifically noting that completion of the line would make Yellowstone "speedily accessible" to tourists.

As a scientist, Professor Ferdinand V. Hayden, a geologist and gov-ernment surveyor, found Langford's descriptions of Yellowstone's ther-mal features especially fascinating. Accordingly, he petitioned Congress

Yellowstone's Giant Geyser, from the pages of *Wonderland*, 1900. Courtesy of the Pacific Northwest Collection, University of Washington Libraries, Seattle.

for extra funding to take his own survey into the region during the summer of 1871. Congress agreed and appropriated $40,000 to ensure that the expedition would be the most complete and systematic ever.

Once more, the office of Jay Cooke intervened in planning for the Hayden survey on behalf of the Northern Pacific Railroad. Cooke's office manager, A. B. Nettleton, wrote directly to Hayden to request that Thomas Moran, a landscape artist of growing renown, be permitted to accompany the expedition as a private citizen. "Please understand that we do not wish to burden you with more people than you can attend to," Nettleton began his letter, "but I think that Mr. Moran will be a very desirable addition to your expedition. . . ." On a personal note, Nettleton also stressed that the favor would "be a great accommodation" to Jay Cooke and the interests of the railroad. "[Moran], of course, expects to pay his own expenses, and simply wishes to take advantage of your cavalry escort."

The palatial National Hotel at Mammoth Hot Springs, Yellowstone, shown here at the turn of the century, was constructed in 1883 and later torn down in 1935. From *Wonderland*, 1903.

In reality, Moran needed financial assistance; like Nathaniel P. Langford, his distant benefactor was none other than Jay Cooke, from whom the artist borrowed the five hundred dollars required to supplement his own meager resources. In this manner, Cooke's endorsement (and funds) directly led to the production of Moran's most famous oil painting, *The Grand Canyon of the Yellowstone*, now housed in the National Museum of American Art, Smithsonian Institution, in Washington, D.C.

As late as September 1871, however, when the Hayden Survey returned from the Yellowstone wilderness, no public campaign to protect the region as a national park had yet been formed. For this reason, the Yellowstone campfire story of 1870 is even more suspect. Certainly,

The interior of the Northern Pacific Railroad station at Gardiner, Montana (no longer standing), was itself beautifully representative of the pioneering rustic style of Yellowstone's early buildings. Courtesy of Burlington Northern Inc.

if the explorers of the preceding expedition had pledged themselves to such a grand scheme, they would not have sacrificed another perfect opportunity — in this instance, the publicity generated by the Hayden Survey — to once more introduce the national park idea to the American people. No one came forward, not even Professor Hayden, who had achieved great distinction in the public eye.

Credit for proposing the introduction of legislation to protect Yellowstone as a public park actually rests with officials of the Northern Pacific Railroad project. The clue is to be found in a letter Professor Hayden received on October 28, 1871, from A. B. Nettleton, written on the stationery of Jay Cooke & Co., Bankers, Financial Agents, Northern Pacific Railroad Company. The letter began:

Dear Doctor:
    Judge Kelley has made a suggestion which strikes me as being an excellent one, viz: Let Congress pass a bill reserving the Great Geyser Basin as a public

park forever—just as it has reserved that far inferior wonder the Yosemite valley and big trees. If you approve this would such a recommendation be appropriate in your official report?

Judge Kelley was Congressman William Darrah Kelley of Philadelphia, a prominent Republican sympathetic to Cooke and his railroad enterprises. Kelley learned about Yellowstone through the published congressional report of Lieutenant Gustavus C. Doane, commander of the cavalry escort for the Washburn Expedition. Nettleton's reference to "Yosemite valley and the big trees" was also significant, for it underscored the crucial matter of precedent. In 1864, Congress had granted Yosemite Valley and the Mariposa Grove of giant sequoias to the state of California "for public use, resort, and recreation," to be held "inalienable for all time." Although Yosemite was a state park, its congressional origin was not overlooked by Yellowstone's own champions. Management considerations aside, Nettleton, for one, appreciated that Congress, through the Yosemite grant, had already established a procedure for setting aside unique scenery in the national interest.

Not until Professor Hayden received the letter in question, however, did he or any of the other explorers—including Nathaniel Langford and Cornelius Hedges—actually begin working to have Yellowstone protected as a public park similar to Yosemite. So again, the intervention of the Northern Pacific Railroad, not the latent sympathies of Yellowstone's actual discoverers, was crucial.

From the perspective of the Northern Pacific, the campaign itself was anticlimactic. Having entrusted the idea for a park to Professor Hayden, officials of the railroad stayed out of the limelight on Capitol Hill, confident that Hayden's fame and credibility as a government geologist would guarantee a favorable outcome. They were not to be disappointed, for on March 1, 1872, only three months after being introduced in Congress, the Yellowstone Park Act was signed into law by President Ulysses S. Grant.

Unfortunately for Jay Cooke, his own hopes of opening the Yellowstone country to tourists were dashed by the depression of 1873. Ten years later and under new management, the Northern Pacific Railroad line across Montana and the spur track to Yellowstone, which headed due south from Livingston, were completed. Nevertheless, the initial efforts of Jay Cooke and A. B. Nettleton had clearly been instrumental, first in launching the Yellowstone Park campaign itself, and later,

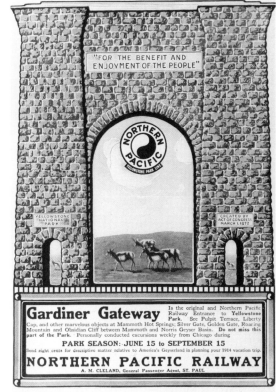

By the turn of the century, the marketing strategy of the Northern Pacific Railroad included the promotion of Yellowstone as a haven for native wildlife. All author's collection.

Designed in the rustic style by Robert C. Reamer, the Old Faithful Inn was completed in 1904 at a cost to the Northern Pacific Railroad of two hundred thousand dollars. Yellowstone National Park photograph (14476). Courtesy of the National Park Service.

in securing public sympathy to retain the park until significant numbers of tourists could in fact begin visiting its wonders.

After 1883, the Northern Pacific Railroad spared no expense to promote Yellowstone National Park. As early as 1886, for example, it underwrote the construction of a series of hotels located near primary attractions. Charles S. Fee, general passenger agent in St. Paul, Minnesota, sought to publicize both the railroad and its accommodations by commissioning a colorfully written and illustrated series of guidebooks, beginning with his personal compilation, *Northern Pacific Railroad: The Wonderland Route to the Pacific Coast, 1885.*

By utilizing quotations from articulate travelers and well-known personalities, these guidebooks introduced Americans not only to Yellowstone, but to Mount Rainier, the Columbia River Gorge, the Cascade Mountains, and similar landmarks made accessible via the Northern Pacific. Even at this early date, Mount St. Helens, visible from the trains approaching Portland, Oregon, was featured for its appeal to observers as "the great Sugar Loaf" of the Pacific Northwest.

Obviously, what modern Americans would recognize as ecological awareness was rarely evident in these guidebook testimonials. After all, the primary objective was to publicize those features of the West which were experiencing growing popularity among tourists. More visitors, in turn, promised the Northern Pacific Railroad greater revenues from hotels, transcontinental trains, and its other passenger-related operations.

Commercial motives aside, the long-range impact of this publicity on the preservation movement in the United States was positive and significant. The railroad's dependence on unspoiled scenery to attract tourists tempered its purely extractive aims, such as logging, mining, and land development. The passenger department, at the very least, became one of the first and most outspoken defenders of Yellowstone National Park. Barely had the railroad come to the gates of the wonderland than Charles S. Fee declared on behalf of his employers:

> We do not want to see the Falls of the Yellowstone driving the looms of a cotton factory, or the great geysers boiling pork for some gigantic packing-house, but in all the native majesty and grandeur in which they appear to-day, without, as yet, a single trace of that adornment which is desecration, that improvement which is equivalent to ruin, or that utilization which means utter destruction.

As if to underscore the pledge, in 1893 the Northern Pacific adopted a new logo, patterned after the Chinese yin-yang symbol of the balanced universe, and suspended it above the caption, "Yellowstone Park Line."

By the turn of the century, as interest in wildlife conservation grew in importance, representatives of the Northern Pacific again spoke out strongly in defense of Yellowstone. More Americans now recognized that the protection of natural wonders, as opposed to wild animals, required only limited amounts of land. Wildlife populations paid no heed to park boundaries laid out to preserve scenery, but instead seasonally followed their traditional migration routes. For the first time, Yellowstone's ecological shortcomings were dramatically apparent. Despite its great size, the park lacked sufficient territory to protect its larger mammals, particularly elk, deer, and antelope. Every autumn, as these species deserted the park for their winter ranges in the lower elevations, they were forced to run a gauntlet of poachers and sportsmen who had no respect for bag limits. For Yellowstone to support its native wildlife effectively, either the park would have to be greatly enlarged or the animals themselves better protected when wandering outside its borders.

The Northern Pacific, through another of its authors, Olin D. Wheeler, enthusiastically supported both park expansion and wildlife protection measures. "In order ... to properly preserve these fast-disappearing relics of wild animal life to future generations," Wheeler wrote in the *Wonderland* guidebook for 1902, "additional territory should be added either to the park proper or to the forest reserve about it, so that absolute protection can be maintained...." Poachers and "game hogs" cared "only for their own selfish pleasure in killing as many deer or elks as they can," he bitterly noted. Perhaps the only solution lay in "the boys and girls" of America, those with the greatest stake in the destiny of Yellowstone. Wheeler concluded that from their "irresistible" efforts, their "vim and enthusiasm," might spring the "national movement," a movement that would finally compel Congress to "arrange for game protection in the Yellowstone Park region for all future time."

Actually, another half century would pass before the addition of Jackson Hole to Grand Teton National Park, lying just to the south, complemented Yellowstone as a wildlife preserve. Again, the delay did not compromise the significance of that first crucial step—of stating unequivocally the need for park expansion. Through its agent, Olin D. Wheeler, the Northern Pacific Railroad fully shared in the credit for that endorsement.

Meanwhile, the national park idea was winning converts nation-wide; at the turn of the century, Mount Rainier in Washington state was among the natural wonders proposed for park status. The Northern Pacific Railroad played a major role in establishing this reserve as well. Approved by Congress in 1899, the park was carved from square-mile sections on the peak; alternate sections were owned by the Northern Pacific, and the balance by the federal government. The railroad's sections dated back to its original land grant, awarded in 1864. Agreeing that these properties were best suited for scenic enjoyment, the government exchanged with Northern Pacific federally held public lands elsewhere in the Pacific Northwest.

The merits of the exchange were somewhat controversial, however. Historians have noted, for example, that the railroad seemed eager to forfeit its commercially worthless holdings on Mount Rainier, especially in light of the richly forested lands received in exchange for the peak. It is also probable, of course, that without the exchange there would not have been a park of any kind, at least not as early as 1899. Instead, much like the modern example of Mount St. Helens, Mount Rainier also would have entered the twentieth century as a checkerboard of properties. Because of the exchange, Mount Rainier was

The establishment of Mount Rainier National Park in 1899 gave added incentive to railroad promotion of the Pacific Northwest. From *Wonderland*, 1898.

spared any possible conflicts over jurisdiction and, subsequently, it became a national park that much sooner.

Irrespective of how Mount Rainier won national park status, the Northern Pacific had long promoted it as a popular tourist attraction, especially through company advertising and the *Wonderland* series. Actual development of the park fell to the Chicago, Milwaukee & Puget Sound Railway, which incorporated the Tacoma Eastern Railroad on July 14, 1890, intending to tap the rich lumber, mineral, and agricultural resources of the surrounding region. The depression of 1893 effectively suspended the project; when construction finally resumed at the turn of the century, Mount Rainier was a national park, adding tourists to the list of potential railroad commodities. The Tacoma Eastern, as the Milwaukee Road's subsidiary, followed the lead of the Northern Pacific at Yellowstone in developing Mount Rainier's primary attractions for the expected surge in visitation.

For obvious reasons, however, primarily because of the sheer number and stunning diversity of its natural wonders, Yellowstone remained

Meeting Yellowstone-bound passengers at Gardiner Gateway was almost certain to be a scene of frenzied activity. *Top.* Motor stages await a rush of excited visitors as a Northern Pacific train pulls to a stop at the station, ca. 1920. *Bottom.* A fleet of park buses prepares to board three hundred college students arriving at Gardiner to take summer jobs in Yellowstone Park hotels, lodges, and camps, ca. 1940. Both courtesy of Burlington Northern Inc.

The New Yakima Gateway to
RAINIER NATIONAL PARK

The Northern Pacific Railroad commissioned this painting (ca. 1930) by the American artist Sydney M. Laurence to promote additional services to Mount Rainier National Park. As a poster, the painting saw wide distribution in stations, ticket offices, and regional hotels. Poster size 30 by 40 inches. Courtesy of Old Seattle Paperworks.

the most popular destination for railroad travelers well into the twentieth century. And that meant trying to wrest patronage from the Northern Pacific Railroad, which still enjoyed all of the advantages of having arrived first on the scene. Between 1883 and 1902, tourists detrained several miles north of the park at Cinnabar, Montana; by 1903 the spur line from Livingston had been extended to the park boundary at Gardiner. From there, it was only five miles by stagecoach to Mammoth Hot Springs, the first of the grand hotels on the park circuit. The Gardiner depot, designed by the Seattle architect Robert C. Reamer, was itself a striking combination of rustic logs, massive stone fireplaces, and high, beamed ceilings. But then, everything had to be first class, for only the wealthy could begin to afford the extravagance of traveling in a transcontinental Pullman or lounging in luxury hotels.

Democracy in the form of the automobile eventually would clamor at the gates of Yellowstone; before middle-class Americans took over the national parks, however, these scenic wonders would first be usurped by the railroads on behalf of their well-to-do clientele. Of the 51,895 visitors who entered Yellowstone during the summer of 1915, for example, fully 44,477 arrived by rail as opposed to only 7,418 by car. Just fifteen years later, however, the proportion had been completely reversed. In 1930 only 26,845 people used the rail entrances into Yellowstone in contrast to the 194,771 who entered by private automobile.

By 1930 no less than five major railroads served Yellowstone and its immediate vicinity. The last to make a concerted effort to increase patronage was the Chicago, Milwaukee, and St. Paul, which in 1926

A 1915 Northern Pacific brochure cover, "Pacific Coast Attractions," highlights the beauty, comfort, and convenience of the Yellowstone Park Line. Courtesy of the California State Railroad Museum, Sacramento.

developed the Gallatin Gateway in Montana as another alternative to existing points of entry. The Milwaukee Road's continuing interest, despite the competition of the automobile, is easily explained. Simply, although the proportion of rail travelers declined in comparison to auto vacationers, by 1925 the actual number of railroad patrons had recovered to its pre-World War I average. Until the Great Depression tightened its grip on rail passenger traffic in the early 1930s, approximately 40,000 people annually still went to "Wonderland" by train. No motivation among the western railroads for seeking to duplicate this ridership elsewhere was more compelling than the example set by the Northern Pacific—catalyst of the national park idea and first monopolizer of the "Yellowstone Park Line."

The *Wonderland* guidebooks, published annually by the Northern Pacific Railroad, featured articles and photographs of western scenery and train travel. In the *Wonderland* cover for 1897, "Liberty" and the eagle float serenely above the Grand Canyon and Lower Falls of the Yellowstone River. The 1899 cover symbolizes the bountiful harvests made possible by the presence of the railroad. Courtesy of the Pacific Northwest Collection, University of Washington Libraries, Seattle.

Top. Thomas Moran's, *Grand Canyon of Arizona from Hermit Rim Road*, chromolithograph (1913), 26¼ by 35 inches. Author's collection. As a painting, this image formed the nucleus of the Santa Fe (now Burlington Northern Santa Fe) Railway's Collection of Southwestern Art. *Bottom.* Opened January 14, 1905, El Tovar Hotel (after the Spanish explorer Pedro de Tovar) testifies to the elegance of the Santa Fe Railway's promotion of Grand Canyon, established as a national park in 1919. Painting by Louis Akin (1907), courtesy of Burlington Northern Santa Fe.

THREE ✣

PRESERVATION EXPRESS
Glacier, the Grand Canyon,
and the National Park Service

I believe [in] the creation of a bureau of national parks. I am of the firm opinion that nothing will be achieved, or practically nothing worth while, until we have such a bureau—until we have men in this bureau whose whole time is taken up with matters pertaining to transportation, to hotels, and to the advancement of the national parks as a whole.

James Hughes, General Passenger Agent, Chicago,
Milwaukee & Puget Sound Railway, 1912

Soon after the turn of the century, every major western railroad was playing a crucial role in the establishment, protection, and improvement of national parks. The managers of these lines were motivated more by a desire to promote tourism and increase profits than by altruism and environmental concern. Nevertheless, preservationists like John Muir came to recognize the value of forming an alliance with a powerful corporate group committed to similar goals, if not from similar ideals. Tourism at the time, however encouraged, provided the national parks with a solid economic justification for their existence. No argument was more vital in a nation still unwilling to pursue scenic preservation at the cost of business achievement.

The Northern Pacific, as the first company to become involved with the national parks, set an example for the other railroads to follow. Across the West, railroad companies learned to appreciate the publicity and profits that could be won by sponsoring scenic preservation in their particular spheres of influence. Among the earliest to respond to the opportunity was the Southern Pacific Railroad in California, which lobbied in 1890 for the establishment of Yosemite, Sequoia, and General Grant national parks, all located in the High Sierra. "Even the soulless Southern Pacific R.R. Co., never counted on for anything

CALIFORNIA
The Home of the Big Tree

THE famous Big Tree, in the Mariposa Grove, near Yosemite Valley, is 400 feet high. Scientists say its age exceeds **9,000 years.** If placed at the junction of Fifth Avenue and Broadway it would fill Broadway and overtop the new **Flatiron Building** by 114 feet. Cut into one-inch boards it would entirely sheath the building on all sides. ❧ ❧ ❧ ❧

For literature and information concerning the **Mariposa Big Tree Grove, Yosemite Valley,** famous **Hotel Del Monte,** and other **Pacific Coast Resorts,** address the

SOUTHERN PACIFIC

Boston, 170 Washington Street; Baltimore, 109 East Baltimore Street; New York City, 349 and 1 Broadway; Syracuse, 129 South Franklin Street; Philadelphia, 109 South Third Street
L. H. NUTTING, G. E. P. A., New York City
E. O. McCORMICK, P. T. M., San Francisco, Cal.   T. J. ANDERSON, G. P. A., Houston, Tex.

This 1904 advertisement informed easterners about the natural wonders of the West by comparing the exaggerated height of the Wawona Tunnel Tree with the famous Flatiron Building in New York City. Reprinted by permission of the Southern Pacific Transportation Company.

good, helped nobly in pushing the bill for [Yosemite] park through Congress." With these words, John Muir recorded the initial astonishment among preservation interests.

Indeed, the company rose to become one of the most vigorous sponsors of protecting natural scenery in general and the West Coast national parks in particular. In 1898, for example, the Southern Pacific's passenger department was the original founder of *Sunset* magazine, a monthly periodical designed expressly to entice settlement and tourism to states served by the railroad, especially California. Each issue contained lavish illustrations, highly descriptive articles, and romantic advertisements promoting Yosemite Valley, the giant sequoias, and other national park attractions accessible via Southern Pacific passenger trains. One of the most popular subjects for photographers was the Wawona Tunnel Tree in Yosemite's Mariposa Redwood Grove. With such wonders of nature to induce travel, the Southern Pacific Railroad profited from the national parks of California for many years.

The Grand Canyon of Arizona provided the Atchison, Topeka & Santa Fe Railway with a similar golden opportunity. Travel to the canyon was considerably improved with the completion in 1901 of a spur track to the South Rim from Williams, Arizona, a distance of approximately sixty miles. Visitors were no longer forced to endure long and tiring stagecoach rides in the desert heat. Similarly, in January 1905, the Santa Fe dedicated its luxurious El Tovar Hotel, also on the canyon brink. Here, too, the publicity of the railroad and its structural improvements contributed immeasurably to the protection of the Grand Canyon, for not until 1908 was it set aside as a national monument by order of President Theodore Roosevelt.

The Santa Fe Railway expected the national monument to focus greater attention on the Grand Canyon and, like the designation of Yellowstone as a "national park," to arouse the curiosity of literally millions of Americans. If these competing western railroads were to approach either the success or the prestige of the Northern Pacific, then Yellowstone was the model they had to recreate.

No railroad, however, was more determined to compete with its rivals than the Great Northern Railway. Completed in 1893 by James J. Hill, it paralleled the Northern Pacific from Minnesota to Washington, except that Hill chose a right-of-way much closer to the Canadian border. As a result, the Great Northern bypassed the Yellowstone country by more than two hundred miles and instead pierced the

The alpine splendor of Swiftcurrent Lake in Glacier National Park inspired
the Great Northern Railway to design the Many Glacier Hotel reminiscent
of a lodge in Switzerland. Courtesy of Burlington Northern Inc.

jagged ranges of the Rocky Mountains in the northwestern corner of
Montana.

As early as 1901, the noted explorer and sportsman, George Bird
Grinnell, endorsed government protection of this region as a forest
preserve, describing it for *Century Magazine* as "the Crown of the
Continent." "Here," he observed, "are cañons deeper and narrower
than those of the Yellowstone, mountains higher than those of the
Yosemite." In other words, properly protected and developed, the territory was equally worthy of national park status. James J. Hill,
renowned for his skepticism about rail passenger service, did not seem
very interested. Then, in 1907, his son, Louis W. Hill, was appointed
president of the Great Northern Railway. Louis, on the other hand, did
sense this magnificent opportunity: after all, immediately south of the
region Grinnell had described ran the tracks of the railroad's main line.

Top. Since 1913, this view of the Glacier Park Lodge from East Glacier Park Station has been the first impression of the region for two million rail visitors. The site, which is just outside the park, was purchased from the Piegan Indians. Hileman photograph (79G-29A-1). Courtesy of the National Archives. *Above left.* The original interior of the Glacier Park Lodge was a colorful hodgepodge of Native American and Oriental motifs, intended to vindicate the claims of the Great Northern Railway that its main line to the Pacific was a natural gateway to the Far East. Hileman photograph (79G-29A-5). Courtesy of the National Archives. *Above right.* From 1927, these alpine adventurers now seem to suggest Julie Andrews's opening scene in the movie "Sound of Music." Reprinted by permission of Burlington Northern Inc.

As president of the Great Northern Railway, Louis W. Hill (left) was instrumental in the development and promotion of Glacier National Park. Hill poses beside the Glacier Park Lodge at East Glacier Park Station, ca. 1920. Courtesy of Burlington Northern Inc.

The following year, Congress began debating the merits of a national park bill. As prospects for its passage improved, Hill's initial interest swelled into unbridled enthusiasm. For years, the Montana Rockies had been out of reach to all but a few hardy sportsmen. Now that a national park might actually hug the tracks of the Great Northern, this trickle of visitors could conceivably be turned into a flood. Perhaps, Hill mused, even Yellowstone might be forced to sacrifice some of its popularity to its newest competitor. Meanwhile, as part of his railroad's ongoing "See America First" campaign, Hill noted that Americans were encouraged to spend their travel dollars elsewhere—in the Swiss Alps or the Canadian Rockies, for example—simply because equally spectacular landscapes at home were not properly protected and promoted.

Swayed by the argument, Congress approved and, in May of 1910, the president signed the act establishing Glacier National Park. With the park itself a reality, Hill's next course of action was obvious: he must do everything possible to provide for the accommodation of visitors. Personally, he did not care to commit the Great Northern both to the construction and operation of a hotel chain. At best, the park season would be only three months long; the project offered little prospect of breaking even on such a substantial capital investment. Yet, Hill realized that he had little choice. Luxury accommodations were the prerequisite for attracting visitors to the national parks, especially in the days before the widespread use of automobiles, when only wealth-ier Americans could afford a vacation in the West. In any case, every extra passenger who filled an otherwise empty seat on one of the rail-road's existing transcontinental trains would represent a net profit, inasmuch as the costs of operating a train were unchanged regardless of the number of people using the system.

In addition to the practical considerations that inevitably crossed Hill's mind, there loomed an equally compelling vision. Louis W. Hill took great personal pride in opening Glacier National Park as his own unique gift to the nation. From the outset, visitors to the park detected his dedication to the project. Mary Roberts Rinehart, for example, writing for *Collier's* magazine, informed her readers in 1916: "Were it not for the Great Northern Railway, travel through Glacier Park would be practically impossible." Of course, the railroad was "not entirely altruistic," the popular novelist confessed, "and yet I believe that Mr. Louis Warren Hill, known always as 'Louie' Hill, has had an ideal and followed it—followed it with an enthusiasm that is contagious."

Proof of her contention could be seen throughout the backcountry, where Hill had scattered a striking assortment of Swiss-style alpine chalets. But nowhere was his commitment more grandly displayed than at East Glacier Park Station and Many Glacier, on the banks of Swift-current Lake. At these locations, dipping lavishly into regional

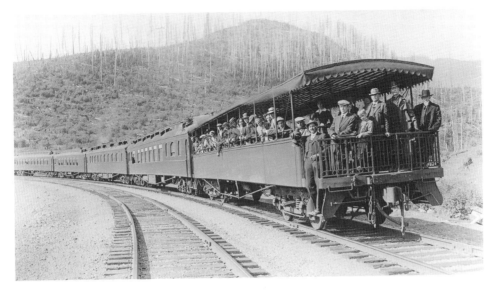

Seasonally, beginning in the summer of 1915, the Great Northern Railway added open observation cars to its transcontinental trains to provide unobstructed views of Glacier National Park. Courtesy of Burlington Northern Inc.

Train time at East Glacier Park Station, 1934. Although it is the height of the Great
Depression, the westbound *Empire Builder* has a good load of passengers. George A. Grant
photograph. Courtesy of the National Park Service.

resources of timber and stone, Hill had personally supervised the construction of two sprawling, rustic hotels, each constituting a $500,000
investment. "Glacier Park Hotel . . . is almost as large as the National
Capitol at Washington," Rinehart observed, displaying a slight tendency to exaggerate. Still, the structure was impressive, and in
combination with its counterpart at Many Glacier, it moved her to reemphasize that the management of the Great Northern Railway "has
done more than anything else to make the park possible for tourists."

Although as much credit could be given to any of the other western
railroads, Hill devoted a unique degree of personal involvement to the
national parks. His spirit fired the national preservation movement at
this very critical juncture in its history. His efforts to improve Glacier
coincided with a two-fold campaign to protect the national parks from
damaging encroachments and, equally important, to establish a
National Park Service. In California, preservationists had just lost a
bitter fight to save the Hetch Hetchy Valley within Yosemite National
Park from being turned over to the city of San Francisco for its munic-
ipal water supply. The loss of Hetch Hetchy's inviting meadows and

woodlands to a dam and reservoir stunned the Sierra Club and its supporters; never before, they concluded, had the need been more critical for a National Park Service to defend the land.

Under the existing arrangement, the Department of the Interior, the War Department, and the U.S. Forest Service all shared responsibility for managing the reserves. No single, centralized federal agency had the power to protect the national parks as a system. But how, preservationists asked themselves, could such an agency be established, especially over the objections of existing federal departments, each jealous of its own authority?

Meanwhile, preservationists were confronted by a powerful numbers argument. Proponents of the Hetch Hetchy dam had been quick to point out that only a few hundred "nature lovers" enjoyed the valley during the summer months; in contrast, fully half a million San Franciscans would benefit year-round from the reservoir. Lacking a rationale whose emotional appeal was equally persuasive, preservationists found themselves in an extremely vulnerable position. The geography of tourism was also against them. Every national park, including Yosemite, was in the West, far removed from the centers of population. Finally, only a few Americans were sympathetic with purely ecological justifications for scenic preservation. John Muir, whose California-based Sierra Club led the fight against the dam, concluded sadly: "Nothing dollarable is safe, however guarded."

Only the railroads, whose own desire to boost travel to the national parks did not materially compromise their scenic integrity, seemed even remotely sympathetic with preservationist ideals. It followed that preservation groups needed to strengthen their ties with the railroads. Richard B. Watrous, secretary of the American Civic Association, and Allen Chamberlain, a leading activist of the Appalachian Mountain Club, were among the first to publicize the advantages of such an alliance. According to Chamberlain, the Hetch Hetchy debate was an especially compelling example of the need to work even harder "to stimulate public interest in the national parks by talking more about their possibilities as vacation resorts." Only if more Americans "could be induced to visit these scenic treasure houses," he concluded, would the public "come to appreciate their value and stand firmly in their defense."

Groping for his own analogy, Watrous decided that tourism might best be defined as the "dignified exploitation of our national parks."

Stephen T. Mather, as first director of the National Park Service, worked closely with railroad executives to improve passenger services throughout the West. In this view, he stands above the "drumhead" of the observation car of the *North Coast Limited*, the premier passenger train of the Northern Pacific Railroad, ca. 1925. Photograph (79-PGN-385), courtesy of the National Archives.

Accordingly, in 1911, he urged preservation groups nationwide to publicize "the direct material returns that will accrue to the railroads, to the concessionaires, and to the various sections of the country that will benefit by increased travel." The railroads' support, he concluded, was particularly "essential" as "one of those practical phases of making the aesthetic possible."

It remained for Secretary of the Interior Walter L. Fisher to give these views the sanction of the government. In September of 1911, he convened a special national parks conference at Yellowstone to discuss the major problems facing the reserves. When several prominent executives of the western railroads, including Louis W. Hill of the Great Northern, accepted Fisher's invitation to attend, preservationists were convinced they were being heard. Fisher's introductory remarks were equally heartening. Speaking directly to the railroad executives, he praised their support for the national parks as the highest form of "enlightened selfishness," self-interest of the type entitling it to the "grateful recognition" of all park advocates. One after another, the executives, led by Hill, returned the compliment with further promises to assist the government in upgrading the facilities of the national parks, especially hotels, roads, and trails. As so many preservationists had hoped, the Yellowstone conference of 1911 established beyond a doubt the firm commitment of the western railroads to embark upon national park improvements and publicity campaigns.

The support could not have been more timely; the National Park Service bill, introduced to Congress in 1911, ran into stiff opposition from powerful opponents in the federal bureaucracy. As a result, hearings on the legislation were still being held five years later. Only the endorsement of the western railroads seemed unshaken. Much like the preservationist interests, the railroads looked forward to working with a single government agency, one committed to promoting the parks full-time rather than as a sideline to a more compelling—and often conflicting—management philosophy.

Meanwhile, the railroads engaged in a flurry of national park promotion; as a group, they spent hundreds of thousands of dollars on advertising brochures, complimentary park guidebooks, and full-page magazine spreads, some of which were in dramatic full-color. Fortunately for park visitors, the competition among the railroads was occasionally tempered by some cooperation. With the arrival of the Union Pacific at the western boundary of Yellowstone National Park in 1907, the Northern Pacific Railroad finally lost its monopoly over the area. Similarly, by 1915, the Chicago, Burlington & Quincy had access to Yellowstone via Cody, Wyoming, a two-hour drive due east of the reserve. Thanks in large part to Stephen T. Mather, who, in December of 1914, became the assistant secretary of the interior in charge of national parks, travelers to Yellowstone finally were able to interchange their routes of entry and departure, all on the same railroad ticket.

Mather, who had already made his own fortune in the mining of borax, now rose to the challenge of bringing order to the national park system. As a Californian and a member of the Sierra Club, his business background and conservation experience taught him that publicity was still the key to winning more public support for the reserves. Accordingly, he nurtured the alliance between preservationists and western railroad officials at every opportunity. The lines' financial response continued to be substantial, with the expectation that their investments would stimulate the flow of goodwill in both directions. In this vein, the Santa Fe and Union Pacific railroads jointly spent half a million dollars in 1915 on national park displays at the Panama-Pacific International Exposition in San Francisco. The Union Pacific contributed a full-size replica of the lobby of the Old Faithful Inn and Old Faithful Geyser in Yellowstone: every hour the modeled "wonder" erupted in a jet of water, just like the original more than a thousand miles away. Visitors were obviously delighted by this unusual display, and equally important from the railroad's perspective, the exhibit reminded people of the national parks' beauty and how they might be reached.

Stimulating public awareness of the available transportation to and the extraordinary scenery of national parks was also the purpose of the *National Parks Portfolio*, a stunning publicity volume containing pictures and descriptions of all the major preserves. No less than seventeen of the western railroads contributed $43,000 in 1916 toward publication of the first edition. Afterward, Stephen T. Mather supervised the mailing of 275,000 copies of the collector's item to carefully selected scholars, politicians, chambers of commerce officials, newspaper editors, and other American leaders who were likely to boost the national park idea.

Meanwhile, with the passage of the National Park Service bill still in doubt, preservationists welcomed another major railroad to their

fold of active political allies. This was the Chicago, Burlington & Quincy. The approval in 1915 of Rocky Mountain National Park, sixty miles northwest of the Burlington's terminus in Denver, Colorado, had provided a special incentive for the company to endorse the creation of a National Park Service. The Burlington began to promote Cody, Wyoming, and the Cody Road as the most scenic gateway into Yellowstone. Finally, an agreement with the Great Northern Railway enabled the Burlington to sell through-tickets to landmarks farther west, including Glacier and Mount Rainier national parks.

Similar arrangements among the Burlington's competitors were offered as a sign of good faith, as another expression of their sincere hope that a National Park Service would soon be established. In this new spirit of cooperation, P. S. Eustis, general passenger agent of the Chicago, Burlington & Quincy, concluded five years of hearings on the National Park Service bill before the House Committee on the Public Lands. "We offer every diversity of route possible," he testified, "all on one ticket."

This evocative series of advertisements ran in magazines across the United States during 1926 and 1927. Note the Union Pacific Railroad's attempt to equate the formations of Bryce and Zion with the architectural achievements of Europe and the Orient. Reprinted with permission.

"Make-Believe Land Come True"

See Bryce Canyon — Zion National Park — Cedar Breaks
Prismatic Plains—Kaibab Forest—North Rim Grand Canyon

Galleries of sculpture like this are numerous in Bryce Canyon. Every shade and tint of every color plays over the statues, rock castles and cathedrals crowded in the colossal chasms and canyons of this new vacation wonderland.

Cliff dwellings, Mormon pioneer outposts, wild horses, deer, the rare white-tail squirrels in a forest beautiful as a dream— and sublime Grand Canyon! Where else can you see as much?

Low fares. Through sleeping cars to Cedar City, then complete 5-day motor-bus tour including Kaibab Forest and North Rim Grand Canyon, or shorter 3 or 4-day tours to Zion, Bryce and Cedar Breaks only. Also escorted all-expense tours. Comfortable lodges. A wonderful vacation itself, or an easy side trip in connection with tours to Salt Lake City, Yellowstone, California or Pacific Northwest. Season June 1 to October 1.

Handsome Book in natural colors tells about this new wonderland in Utah-Arizona. Ask for it.

Address nearest Union Pacific Representative, or General Passenger Agent, Union Pacific, (Dept. U) at Omaha, Neb. : Salt Lake City, Utah : Portland, Ore. : Los Angeles, Cal.

UNION PACIFIC

Two additional national park conferences, called in 1913 and 1915 by the Department of the Interior, likewise reaffirmed the unanimous support for a Park Service among the western railroads. The opposition in the federal bureaucracy, once confident of success, could no longer withstand this powerful tide of enthusiasm from such a prestigious quarter. On August 25, 1916, preservationists cleared their last potential hurdle when President Woodrow Wilson signed the National Park Service Act into law.

In recognition of his many contributions to the national parks in his capacity as assistant secretary of the interior, Stephen T. Mather was appointed the first director of the new organization. With the National Park Service a reality, he now turned his attention to park system additions and improvements. Mather was particularly concerned about the Southwest, where scenic magnificence was represented by only one major reserve, the Grand Canyon. Subsequently, in 1919, he won approval for Zion National Park, the spectacular gorge in southern Utah renowned as "The Yosemite of the Desert." Bryce Canyon, a neighboring wonderland of fanciful spires and sandstone gargoyles, eventually received park status in 1924.

Neither area, however, had adequate roads or overnight accommodations. Cedar Breaks, soon to become the breathtaking national monument between Bryce and Zion, and the North Rim of the Grand Canyon, approximately one hundred miles to the south, were in the same predicament. To alleviate these problems of transportation and lodging, Mather approached the president and board of directors of the Union Pacific Railroad and asked them to take charge of the needs of tourists throughout the entire region.

The Union Pacific, despite some initial reluctance to commit itself to such a substantial investment, eventually responded with everything Mather had hoped for—and more. Accompanied by widespread advertising campaigns in the best tradition of national park promotion, the railroad constructed a new branch line from Lund, on the Los Angeles/Salt Lake City main line, over to Cedar City, just north of Zion. At Cedar City, passengers transferred to company-supplied buses for package tours of all four of the area's "wonderlands." To accommodate the many expected guests, the Union Pacific constructed lodges and cabins in each reserve. The most elegant of these buildings, the Grand Canyon Lodge on the North Rim, was dedicated in 1928. For the first time since 1905, when the Santa Fe Railway

Passengers departing Union Pacific company hotels in the Southwest were treated to employee "sing aways." Here the staff of the Bryce Canyon National Park Lodge sings good-bye to guests in the summer of 1940. Courtesy of the Union Pacific Railroad Company Museum, Omaha, Nebraska.

opened the El Tovar on the South Rim, both sides of the canyon had comparable service.

"Our relations with the parks are naturally very close, and I believe they should be closer," said Louis W. Hill in defense of his own $1.5 million investment in Glacier National Park. In fact, his hotels and chalets, assigned to the railroad's subsidiary, Glacier Park, Inc., were not sold until 1961. Managed today by the Greyhound Corporation, the buildings are still there, rising against their mountain backgrounds, blending the man-made with the natural in a fitting memorial to Hill's idealism and philanthropy.

Stephen Mather's death in 1930 brought to an end more than two decades of dedicated involvement with America's national parks, yet his primary goal to increase park visitation had been achieved. More than three million people traveled through the national parks and monuments that year, almost a tenfold increase since he had taken office as director of the National Park Service. Railroad executives applauded his success, as did most preservationists, who rejoiced in the security that popularity brought to the scenic reserves.

The alliance forged by the western railroads, preservation groups, and the National Park Service survived intact for the next quarter century. As late as 1960, the pages of *Holiday*, *National Geographic*, and similar magazines sparkled with advertisements depicting the joys of rediscovering the West by rail, especially by visiting the national parks. On the Santa Fe Railway, for example, the streamliner *Grand Canyon*

Dedicated in 1928, the Union Pacific lodge on the North Rim of the Grand Canyon further testified to the railroad's immersion in promoting the national parks. Courtesy of the Union Pacific Railroad Museum, Omaha, Nebraska.

provided daily service between Chicago and Los Angeles, with through-cars to the canyon by way of the spur track from Williams, Arizona. Similarly, the Union Pacific added the *National Parks Special* for seasonal traffic to Zion, Bryce, and the Grand Canyon; it also expanded service to include the *Yellowstone Special*, whose summer runs ferried patrons between West Yellowstone and connecting main line trains at Salt Lake City.

For this legacy to have survived into the modern era, passenger trains in the West would have had to dramatically increase their patronage. Instead, the passenger business barely broke even during the 1960s as the federal government invested billions of dollars in competing highways and airports rather than in railroad facilities. In addition, many of the railroads in the East were dismantling their passenger operations, depriving trains in the West of vital connections with major population centers. Consequently, the promotion of the national parks by the western railroads no longer seemed justified, and public awareness about that unique relationship and its history finally dimmed.

Once again end of the track for the Grand Canyon Railway, the El Tovar Hotel, shown here in 1936, overlooks the depths of Arizona's renowned chasm. George A. Grant photograph (910). Courtesy of the National Park Service.

Evidence during the early 1980s pointed to the restoration of rail transportation in the United States, not only between major cities, but to the national parks as well. Preservation groups were especially heartened in 1983 by the announcement that a private developer intended to purchase and rehabilitate the Santa Fe Railway branch line between Williams, Arizona, and the South Rim of the Grand Canyon. As late as August 1983 it appeared that the track would be torn up for scrap; finally, in the railroad's eleventh hour, a proposal for saving the branch line was endorsed by the Santa Fe Railway, the developer, and the town of Williams.

For its part, the Santa Fe Railway agreed to sell the tracks to the developer, Charles Newman, president of Railroad Resources Inc., for approximately three million dollars. Meanwhile, Williams agreed to allow Railroad Resources Inc., to construct a hotel complex within the community as part of a twenty million dollar project to connect Williams, the Grand Canyon airport, and facilities at the South Rim via the railroad. Early plans for the railroad itself called for purchasing a steam locomotive and vintage heavyweight passenger cars to ferry hotel patrons between Williams and the canyon rim.

Environmentalists, concerned about overcrowding in the national parks, greeted the announcement as a vindication of their contention that all future development of visitor services and overnight accommodations should occur outside the parks rather than next to their primary attractions. Similarly, rail passenger lobbyists endorsed the restoration as part of their own campaign to rehabilitate the rail passenger network dismantled throughout the United States during the 1960s. In this spirit both environmentalists and rail passenger advocates looked forward to another "pragmatic alliance," a union whose historical significance seemed on the verge of renewed importance in the pending resurrection of the route of the *Grand Canyon* to its former glory.

FOUR ⊗

YOSEMITE VALLEY
RAILROAD *Highway of*
History, Pathway of Promise

Up its matchless canyon this new trail toils, unfolding moment by moment one of the most pic-turesque series of mountain pictures that nature has fashioned in her whole wide world. This little piece of railroad is sure to take a leading place among the few famous scenic railways of the world.

Lanier Bartlett, *Pacific Monthly*, 1907

Among wilderness enthusiasts and rail fans alike, few proposals over the years have aroused greater appeal than calls for rebuilding the Yosemite Valley Railroad. Granted, some purists might still be opposed, as was the case following its completion in May 1907. "In California and the far West, there are people who insist that here-after the great valley is to be a mere picnic-ground with dancing plat-forms, beery choruses, and couples contorting in the two-step." So confessed a reporter for *Cosmopolitan* magazine, summing up the belief that "the Black Cavalry of Commerce has been sent out to trample down the fairy rings." Allegedly, such disgruntlement could still be traced to "nature cranks" and the "athletic rich," those resentful that Yosemite was no longer exclusively their domain. "There is the railroad into Yosemite," the reporter concluded, declaring democracy victori-ous, "and all the arguments since Adam and Eve will not put it away."

In fact, the Yosemite Valley Railroad did not enter the valley proper, or for that matter the national park. Nor would it last even forty years, let alone rival the story of Adam and Eve. Reportedly bankrupt in 1944, the railroad would be auctioned the following year and immedi-ately scrapped. Today, only crumbling embankments lining the Merced River remind anyone that a railroad was ever there. If only it had sur-vived, its lingering champions still protest, it might have relieved over-crowding in Yosemite, ideally through an extension to the valley floor.

The Yosemite Valley featured this illustration on the cover of its promotional brochure for the 1928 travel season. Courtesy of the Yosemite National Park Research Library.

Otherwise, its demise was a foregone conclusion, chiefly ordained by America's growing preference for the automobile and the declining fortunes of its shippers. Although famed for carrying tourists, it also transported a variety of raw materials, including logs cut from the forests bordering Yosemite National Park. Initially reserved inside the boundary, in February 1905 those forests were largely written out, removing the last hurdle to those bent on making a fortune from their prized stands of sugar pine.

Construction on the railroad began shortly afterwards, in September 1905, following a right-of-way seventy-eight miles east by northeast through the Sierra Nevada foothills from Merced to El Portal. Much to the railroad's advantage, the Merced River Canyon already provided a means for penetrating deep into the mountains. Only east of El Portal did the park and a steeper ascent finally block the way. Here the railroad spent $100,000 to provide a wagon road (now known as the Arch Rock entrance), transferring passengers to company-owned stages for the remaining twelve miles to the valley floor.

Pullman Service *All the Way*

YOSEMITE CARS

The end of your railroad journey and the entrance to the magic valley — that is El Portal. Here is the terminal station of Yosemite Valley Railroad, a distinctive rustic structure blending admirably with the rugged setting.

As the train nears Yosemite Valley, the view becomes ever more magnificent. Just before reaching El Portal—the river rushing by at our feet—in the hazy distance, a silvery shimmering streak breaking the rugged cliffs. It is Chinquapin Falls, first to be seen of the waterfalls of Yosemite—a promise of the scenic glories soon to be unfolded.

YOSEMITE VALLEY RAILROAD CO.

This page from the Yosemite Valley Railroad's 1928 travel brochure, "Yosemite via Merced Canyon Route," featured the station platform at El Portal. Courtesy of the Yosemite National Park Research Library.

Destroyed by fire on October 27, 1917, the Del Portal Hotel enjoyed but a brief decade of service. Courtesy of the Yosemite National Park Research Library.

Undoubtedly, in Europe the road itself would have been a cog-assisted railway, engineered both for making the grade while harmonizing with the landscape. Simply, Europe had taken a different turn, tackling foremost the density of its population. Switzerland, for example, was developing narrow-gauge, electric railroads capable of climbing high into the Alps. It seemed perfectly logical to bring in mountain railroads; after all, the Alps had been settled for a thousand years. Besides, the Swiss were committed to developing railroads that were also recognized as works of art.

In marked contrast, the United States resisted rail-based transportation inside the national parks, considering railroads, as a part of industry, much too dingy and invasive. Obviously, the intimacy and aesthetics of European technology did not translate to the United States. Bigger was better than intimate; power and efficiency were preferred to art. Besides, Americans intuitively preferred individualism, their most distinguishing national trait. Why suffer the restrictions of railroad travel as soon as automobiles could provide another way?

Thus the Yosemite Valley Railroad would stop at El Portal rather than climb on to meet its namesake. Regardless, since few cars or highways yet existed, the railroad could only thrive, cutting what used to be two days by stagecoach into but four hours on the train. Obviously, the stage line between Merced and El Portal was rapidly driven out of business. By 1913 motor stages further replaced stagecoaches between El Portal and the valley floor, reducing that leg of the journey from four hours to an hour and a half. For travelers arriving on the evening train, the railroad also constructed Del Portal, a rustic four-story hotel just a short distance from the station. Dedicated in 1907, it burned a decade later, a considerable loss and one the railroad decided not to replace.

In 1904, the Southern Pacific Railroad chose the Wawona Tunnel Tree in Yosemite National Park's Mariposa Redwood Grove for the cover of "Big Trees," an annual promotional brochure. Carved out in 1881, the tree finally toppled during the harsh winter of 1969. Courtesy of the California State Railroad Museum, Sacramento.

Other improvements included an agreement with the Southern
Pacific Railroad for sleeping-car service direct from Los Angeles and
San Francisco. By 1910, first-class passengers in either city could board
the evening train, snuggle comfortably into their berths, and wake up at
El Portal, all without being disturbed to make the transfer at Merced. A
parlor-observation car delighted passengers on the daytime run, and,
during the summer season the railroad added a full-sized diner.

By 1916 the railroad was averaging fourteen thousand passengers,
indeed an important milestone. Even then, however, a disquieting shift
was in the wind. Slightly more people had chosen to come by car, a
phenomenon obviously portending problems for the railroad. Indeed,
the very next year its passenger volume plummeted forty percent, to
only 8,612. In 1918 it got even worse. Fewer than four thousand people saw the Merced River Canyon from the train, despite every effort
to attract more passengers, including a reduction in the standard fare
by three dollars from $18.50.

In contrast, 26,669 people entered Yosemite Valley by car, up from
14,527 and 22,456 in 1916 and 1917, respectively. Clearly, the American love affair with the automobile was well under way. Moreover, the
National Park Service, just established by Congress, had no intentions
of cooling the romance. Government appropriations were all about
numbers, and private cars were obviously to be more popular than
being required to take the train. "The fact that the majority of people
entering the park came in private automobiles," Yosemite's superintendent reported in 1917, for example, "is evidence that it is this class of
travel that must be given the bulk of consideration in future park
development work." Specifically, "roads and public parking places must
be given special consideration by the Service, and garage facilities and
hotel and camp accommodations which appeal to this class of travel
must be maintained by the concessioners."

The assessment appealed even to preservationists, at least in 1917.
Who could have foreseen that Yosemite would close the century with
more than four million visitors annually? Prior to World War I, when
automobiles were first admitted to the national parks, the problem was
a lack of visitors. As late as 1902 Yosemite had only five thousand annually, a figure that barely doubled even in the first years of the railroad.
With good reason, preservationists feared for the integrity of the entire
park system. Congress was not about to support the parks indefinitely
for the benefit of the rich, those fortunate enough to travel first-class

Collector's Portfolio
See America First

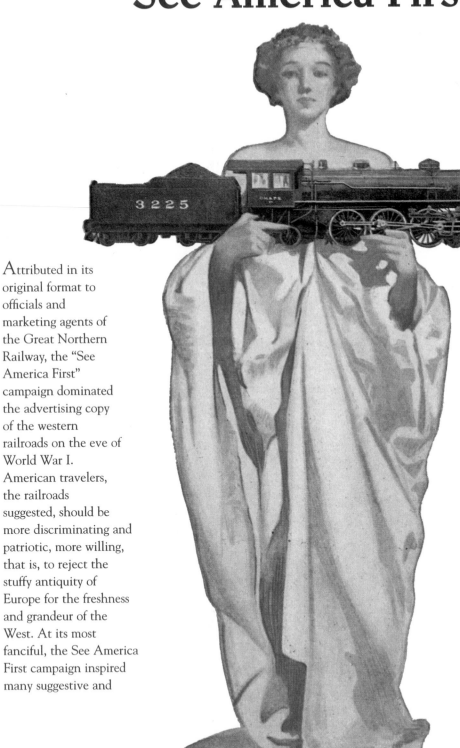

Attributed in its original format to officials and marketing agents of the Great Northern Railway, the "See America First" campaign dominated the advertising copy of the western railroads on the eve of World War I. American travelers, the railroads suggested, should be more discriminating and patriotic, more willing, that is, to reject the stuffy antiquity of Europe for the freshness and grandeur of the West. At its most fanciful, the See America First campaign inspired many suggestive and memorable images, such as this "Madonna of the Rails," reproduced from the title page of the Milwaukee Road's period guidebook, *Across the Continent*. Consider, above all, the intended impression on our forebears, who the railroad likely hoped would recoil from the all-too-common complaint that traveling behind coal-burning locomotives was dirty and uncomfortable. Courtesy of the Pacific Northwest Collection, University of Washington Libraries, Seattle.

The railroad as art—as a technology to be celebrated and admired—is imaginatively revealed in these complementary paintings by the artist Gustav Krollmann. Born and trained in Vienna, Austria, Krollmann emigrated to St. Paul, Minnesota, where he completed these paintings as part of a Northern Pacific poster series unveiled by the railroad between 1930 and 1931. Note the emphasis on the national

parks; other landscapes in the series include Old Faithful Geyser and Mount St. Helens. Contrast Krollmann's style with that of John Fery, whose grand painting immediately follows. Could even the most suggestive video or modern photograph ever match either artist's ability to arouse a longing to see the West before anywhere else? Poster sizes 40 by 30 inches. Both author's collection.

Collector's Portfolio: See America First

First commissioned by the Great Northern Railway in 1910, the artist John Fery is renowned for his pictures of Glacier National Park. The "See America First" ideology of the Great Northern Railway is also beautifully represented in this large Fery Painting, *Mount Index in the Cascades* (Washington State). Note how the coloring between and beside the rails blends perfectly with the roadbed's surroundings. It is as if the rails are but a pathway, just a momentary intrusion on the ancient mountain wilderness. So too

the locomotive, although the center of attention, is small and indistinct. In this fashion, landscape artists since the mid-nineteenth century had wrestled with the discomforting thought that "the machine" was in "the garden." Depending on one's interpretation, the train is everything to fear or nothing to fear, but a fleeting incursion on nature or indeed the harbinger of its destruction. Oil on canvas, 47 ¼ by 83 inches. Courtesy of Burlington Northern Santa Fe.

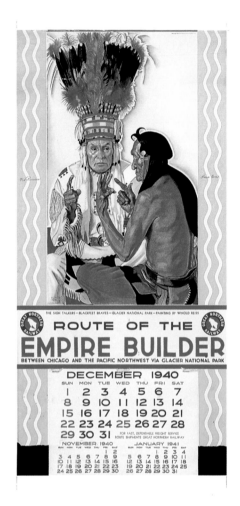

Early in the twentieth century, it was common to think of Native Americans as a "vanishing race." Several of the western railroads, especially the Great Northern and Santa Fe, generously supported artists' and photographers' efforts to record native cultures before they slipped away. Gradually, the depiction of Native Americans in or near national-park settings proved no less irresistible as an important and colorful cornerstone of the See America First campaign. Invariably, such depictions were often idealized, as artists strove to commemorate the Indians' pride and endurance, even in the face of conquest, dispossession, and cultural loss. *Left. The Sign Talkers: No Runner and Hair Coat*, by Winold Reiss. Born in Karlsruhe, Germany, in 1883, Reiss stepped off the train at Glacier National Park during a snowstorm in 1919 and began his life's work, in the Great Northern's words, providing "an opportunity to look into the hearts of a people of the past with sympathetic understanding of their sacrifices to the march of civilization." Original calendar 31 by 16 inches. Author's collection. *Right.* Original magazine advertisement, 1921. Author's collection.

Top. *Indians on Rim of Grand Canyon* (1918), by Eanger Irving Couse. 24 by 28 inches. Courtesy of the Santa Fe Railway Collection of Southwestern Art. *Bottom.* Long a commercial artist for the Santa Fe Railway, Hernando Villa composed this brilliant portrait in 1929 to publicize the railroad's crack limited the *Chief*. Magazine advertisement, reprinted by permission.

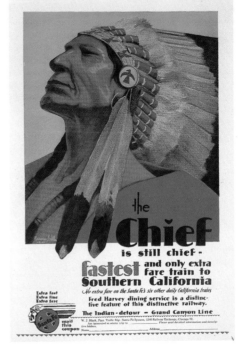

The
Great White
Throne
in
Zion National Park
Southern Utah

See This
Colorful Kingdom of Scenic Splendor

Zion National Park—Bryce Canyon—Cedar Breaks—Red Canyon
Prismatic Plains—Kaibab Forest—North Rim Grand Canyon

"Unique, incomparable, sublime," says Hal Evarts, the noted writer. Mountains glowing red and shining white. Mile-deep canyons filled with mile-high temples! Canyons holding exquisite fairy cities with countless castles, cathedrals, mosques and pagodas of bewildering beauty, tinted with the colors of a glorious sunset. Prismatic plains, cliff dwellings, enchanting forests alive with deer.

Low summer fares. Complete 450-mile 5-day tour including Kaibab National Forest and North Rim Grand Canyon, or shorter 2 or 3-day tours to Zion, Bryce and Cedar Breaks only. Also escorted all-expense tours. Smooth-riding motor busses. Comfortable lodges. A memorable summer vacation in itself or an easy side trip on tours to Salt Lake City, Yellowstone, California or the Pacific Northwest.

Handsome Book in natural colors tells about this new wonderland in Utah-Arizona. Ask for it.

Address nearest Union Pacific Representative, or General Passenger Agent (Dept. A) at Omaha, Neb. :-: Salt Lake City, Utah :-: Portland, Ore. :-: Los Angeles, Cal.

UNION PACIFIC

Should all else fail, the railroads could always count on the monumentalism of the American West to instill potential passengers with curiosity and wanderlust. In Union Pacific country, no landmark was more popular than the Great White Throne in Zion National Park, shown here in an advertisement published in April 1926. Painting signed H. Foster. Shown approximate original size; reprinted with permission.

The majestic backdrop of Glacier National Park and the Middle Fork of the Flathead River inspired this painting commissioned for the unveiling of the 1947 modernization of the Great Northern's famed *Empire Builder*, as featured on the cover of a brochure distributed to boarding passengers. Shown approximate original size; from the collection of Richard Piper.

Collector's Portfolio: See America First

From original painting by ADOLPH HEINZE

THE HIGHWAY NEAR MANY GLACIER HOTEL

Until widespread use of the automobile, travel both at home and abroad was generally limited to the wealthy, for whom the so-called Grand Tour of Europe had long been familiar. Beyond turning the eyes of patriotic tourists away from Europe in the first place, the success of the See America First campaign obviously rested on constant reassurances that the West may be wild yet it was no less accessible, safe, or inviting. Railroad guidebooks, company logos, menu covers, timetables—even luggage stickers and ink blotters—were creatively invoked to portray those all-important scenes of majesty yet serenity, of a comfortable wilderness experience in the companionship of fellow travelers. *Above.* Page from the Great Northern Railway brochure, *The Call of the Mountains,* 1927. Author's collection.

Collector's Portfolio: See America First

This evocative painting by Thomas Moran graced one of a series of Northern Pacific ink blotters. Original approximately letter size. Courtesy of the California State Railroad Museum, Sacramento.

Great Northern Railway luggage sticker, ca. 1925. Original diameter approximately 4½ inches. Author's collection.

The logo of the Tacoma Eastern Railroad featured its popular destination, Mount Rainier. Courtesy of the Pacific Northwest Collection, University of Washington Libraries, Seattle.

Few western railroads could rival the marketing genius of the Southern Pacific. Not content that travelers only see America first, for example, in 1898 the Southern Pacific founded *Sunset* magazine, and immediately filled it with articles, advertisements, and other solicited testimonials extolling both the scenery and natural resources of California and the Far West. Above, the May 1904 cover featured a painting by the artist Chris Jorgensen, showing Half Dome and an Indian woman in Yosemite Valley. Right, an unidentified artist further celebrates the timeless allure of Half Dome for its eager corporate patron, ca. 1910. *Sunset* cover courtesy of Sunset Publishing Company; Half Dome brochure (shown approximate original size) courtesy of the Yosemite National Park Research Library.

The Southern Pacific Railroad commissioned Maurice Logan to paint this colorful view of Emerald Bay at Lake Tahoe. Although several hours north of Yosemite, Lake Tahoe was frequently offered as part of package tours to the national park. Courtesy of the California State Railroad Museum, Sacramento.

and to stay in luxury hotels. At least, every opponent of preservation was learning the persuasiveness of that argument, even if it was meant not to defend the poor but rather to discredit the national parks.

Compounding the problem, every national park was still in the West, far removed from the country's major centers of population. Only the railroads covered such distances swiftly and comfortably, but not at prices within the budget of most American families.

The automobile, on the other hand, promised to "democratize" long-distance travel, finally making the parks accessible to what was increasingly described as America's middle class. It followed that the security of the national parks would be considerably strengthened, both politically and economically. Mounting threats to the national parks, principally from proponents of water power and reclamation projects, further underscored the necessity of compromising some wilderness to accommodate the automobile. Either preservationists conceded additional space for access roads and parking lots, or Congress would force them to live with dams, reservoirs, power lines, and aqueducts. In the end, what other choice did preservationists have if they hoped to maintain the fundamental integrity of the national parks?

Temporarily, at least, the return of national prosperity following World War I was to soften those concerns. Leisure travel boomed, and with it America's railroads. Between 1921 and 1925, the Yosemite Valley Railroad itself averaged twenty thousand passengers annually, restoring confidence that the years ahead would see even stronger gains.

However, by 1928 the number of passengers had fallen by a whopping eighty percent, despite another reduction in the round trip fare to only $10.50. The reason lay on the opposite bank of the Merced River—the new All-Year Highway, completed in 1926. Equally ominous, the relentless cutting of sugar pines in the mountains spelled the beginning of the end of the railroad's logging business. Granted, shipments of trees and other commodities would last into the 1930s. However, the precipitous decline in passengers precluded the luxury of losing any more business, especially given the onset of the Great Depression.

Bankruptcy and reorganization followed, this in 1935. In December 1937 severe flooding tore through major sections of the line. Finally, by 1944, the owners of the railroad had had enough. A few historians speculate that the railroad was still profitable, in effect, that its owners were holding out. In either case, they now petitioned the Interstate Commerce Commission for permission to abandon the entire route.

From the era of the Gibson Girl to the Flapper, Yosemite and Lake Tahoe were California's favorite Sierra Nevada retreats. *Left.* Courtesy of the Bancroft Library. *Center.* Courtesy of the Huntington Library. *Right.* Courtesy of the California State Railroad Museum.

Left: In addition to promoting the national parks of California, the Southern Pacific Railroad supported the establishment of Crater Lake National Park, Oregon, in 1902. Courtesy of the California State Library, Sacramento. *Right:* This luxurious brochure cover, ca. 1920, depicts Cathedral Rocks mirrored in the Merced River of Yosemite Valley. The Indian woman and papoose in the foreground represent the Miwok-Paiute culture indigenous to the region. Courtesy of the California State Library, Sacramento.

Like its competitor, the Southern Pacific Railroad, the Atchison, Topeka, and Santa Fe Railway did not have direct rail service to Yosemite National Park. Instead, both major railroads offered a variety of connecting or subsidiary stage services that linked with their main lines in Fresno and Merced. With the completion of the Yosemite Valley Railroad in 1907, cooperating rail agreements were also finally possible, and both the Southern Pacific and Santa Fe redoubled their Yosemite promotional efforts. Shown here are promotional paintings that were purchased by the Santa Fe. *Above:* "Yosemite Valley" (1907), by J. R. Mersfelder. *Left:* "Yosemite Falls" (1911), by Charles Rogers. Both courtesy of the Santa Fe Railway Company Collection of Southwestern Art.

There were some official protests, most notably by O. A. Tomlinson, regional director of the National Park Service, and Michael W. Straus, the acting secretary of the interior. Secretary Straus personally urged the Interstate Commerce Commission to consider "public convenience and necessity," neither of which "would be served by the abandonment of the Yosemite Valley Railroad." Director Tomlinson was right—the abandonment only portended "a step backward." History alone, Secretary Straus concluded, adding a subtle note of caution, confirmed that "the Yosemite Valley Railroad can perform a needed and valuable service in taking care of visitors to Yosemite National Park."

Unfortunately, there were no passengers currently to prove the argument. World War II still raged in the Pacific, disrupting what little even survived of the railroad's remaining traffic. In peacetime, would Americans return to the trains or go right back to their cars? The ICC agreed it would be the latter, and in June 1945 granted the petition for abandonment, presaging the final trains to run in August. Henceforth, the Yosemite Valley Railroad would live on only in histories tinged with nostalgia and regret.

To be sure, rail enthusiasts still lament the chain of events that cost them one of their favorite mountain railroads. Preservationists would also come to see its abandonment as a consequential loss. As predicted, Yosemite was deprived of a reasonable alternative to the horde of

YOSEMITE VALLEY
and the **BIG TREES**

Glacier Point, 3,250 feet above the Valley.

Southern Pacific

motor vehicles now descending on the park. By 1954 annual visitation topped one million; in 1967 the figure was more than two million. Especially in Yosemite Valley, it seemed that the automobile had gotten entirely out of hand.

Conceding the need for some reforms, in 1968 the Park Service discontinued the popular firefall (burning embers of bark pushed off the cliff at Glacier Point). Three thousand feet below, in Stoneman Meadow, its nightly displays had attracted thousands. Correspondents described the crush of people and cars as reminiscent of a drive-in movie, complete with litter, blaring radios, and after-show traffic jam. Although a century-old tradition, the firefall was hardly a natural feature of Yosemite. It should be stopped, the Park Service agreed, before visitors started thinking only of diversions and amusements.

Bolder still, the next step directly challenged the hegemony of the automobile. In 1970, park officials closed the eastern third of the valley to motorists and, in cooperation with the concessionaire, introduced a system of free public shuttles. Henceforth, only the buses could be used between popular trail heads and other points of interest.

The improvements, although modest, were considered revolutionary at the time. Vegetation returned to trampled meadows; there was more serenity in the evening air. Hikers and bicyclists also welcomed the opportunity to use existing roadways without being intimated by long lines of passing cars. The shuttles themselves became very popular, hailed by a public learning to appreciate their convenience and role in salvaging Yosemite from the congestion of the automobile.

Rallying to the call for a permanent solution, twenty-nine percent of respondents to the General Management Plan called for restoring the Yosemite Valley Railroad, this in 1975. The Park Service strategically demurred, noting the difficulty not only of rebuilding the railroad but also extending it throughout the valley. Instead, new parking lots were seriously considered, either in a remote corner at the west end of the valley or somewhere appropriate just outside. However, opponents were not convinced, charging again that parking lots anywhere close to Yosemite Valley would merely transfer the problem, not resolve it.

Besides, even if shuttles only entered the valley proper, a large number of vehicles would be needed to accommodate the existing crowds, by 1987 surpassing three million every year. Four million were right behind, cresting at that figure in 1994. In the winter of 1997, a devastating flood brought the first significant reprieve from overcrowding in more than fifty years. Even so, the object was never to deny anyone the privilege of seeing Yosemite Valley. Rather, the goal was responsibility, ensuring that whatever the number of visitors, all would enter the park more modestly and unobtrusively.

Accordingly, it remains a problem requiring more than retooling the automobile into buses and shuttle systems. More likely, it means eliminating motor vehicles altogether. As envisioned by Christopher Swan, a planner and entrepreneur based in San Francisco, for example, Yosemite without cars still calls for maximizing light-rail. No other system offers enough capacity while protecting the environment. Following traditional corridors, separate tracks would enter the park from the north, west, and south, then continue as a single line across the valley floor.

The pattern is common in western Europe, where a scarcity of land and overcrowding are daily facts of life. If America is to be as crowded, it must be as receptive to innovation. Simply put, yesterday's future has arrived. Wherever Americans gather, more crowds are now inevitable, and gather Americans will wherever they put a road. Should it not, then, be a railroad instead of another highway? Undoubtedly, the future of Yosemite depends on our willingness to follow the example of other countries already convinced of the proper choice.

After lying dormant for 123 years. Mount St. Helens roared back to life on May 18, 1980. By Austin Post, courtesy of the U.S. Geological Survey.

FIVE ✠

BURLINGTON NORTHERN AND THE LEGACY OF MOUNT ST. HELENS

SEATTLE, May 18—Burlington Northern Inc. today announced it will donate a unique piece of property to the U.S. government—the summit of Mount St. Helens.

Burlington Northern Inc., 1982

The American people, for all their love of Yellowstone, the Grand Canyon, Glacier, and Mount Rainier, have largely forgotten their debt to the railroads of the West for first bringing these and other national parks into the life of the nation. To many, the golden age of rail passenger service died on May 1, 1971, when the National Railroad Passenger Corporation, popularly known as Amtrak, took over the operation of the few surviving long-distance passenger trains in the United States. The railroads themselves, sensing that their future was all in freight traffic, were only too happy to be rid of the responsibility of providing passenger services to the traveling public.

Throughout the 1970s the railroad corporations seemed hardly to notice the significance of their history, even as it pertained to the national parks. Imagine, then, the astonishment that greeted the announcement on May 18, 1982, that Burlington Northern Inc., intended to deed its property on the summit of Mount St. Helens in Washington State to facilitate the establishment of the Mount St. Helens National Volcanic Monument. Two years earlier to the day, early on Sunday morning, May 18, 1980, Mount St. Helens roared back to life with a thundering eruption. The north face of the mountain literally blew itself apart, spewing smoke, ash, and cinders tens of thousands of feet into the atmosphere. Simultaneously, millions of tons of mud, shattered tree trunks, and other debris swept down the northern slope, choking famed Spirit Lake and turning the Toutle River into a boiling, raging torrent.

All told 215 square miles were leveled by the blast, which, although expected for weeks, still took sixty lives among people too close to the mountain. Obviously, no amount of warning had prepared even government agencies to anticipate such a powerful and devastating eruption. Consequently, it was not until months later, when no other major eruptions seemed imminent, that everyone could begin to appreciate the unique opportunity that now presented itself to chronicle the rebirth of the summit and its environs, perhaps by protecting Mount St. Helens as a national monument or park.

The stage was therefore set for Burlington Northern's historic announcement. Burlington Northern Inc., as co-owner with the federal government of Mount St. Helens, was especially committed to the protection of the peak, now a hollowed out, gaping crater 1,313 feet lower in elevation than the original summit. Extending from the lip of the crater, and downslope opposite the blast area, arcing ninety degrees

Northern Pacific Railroad advertisement, 1926, reprinted by permission of Burlington Northern Inc.

Mt. St. Helens from Spirit Lake

In the Glorious Pacific Northwest

A quiet lake, fir-fringed — mirroring a snowy mountain peak. Sunlight glistening on the crest of Mt. St. Helens, and sifting the mysterious shadows of the emerald forests at her feet.

This is but one of the sublime retreats in the Pacific Northwest— the ideal vacation land. I will be glad to send you illustrated booklets that will help you plan your trip.— A. B. S.

"Mount St. Helens from Portland," photo-illustration from *Wonderland*, 1902. Courtesy of the Pacific Northwest Collection, University of Washington Libraries, Seattle.

from due south to due west, lay Burlington Northern's property. Exactly one square mile, the parcel dated back to 1864 and the original land grant awarded to the Northern Pacific Railroad. This portion of the mountain would obviously be the nucleus of the park or interpretive zone proposed by preservationists. As a result, Burlington Northern Inc., decided in 1982 to deed the entire section back to the federal government.

A century ago, when the Northern Pacific Railroad planned its right-of-way across what was then Washington Territory, no one could have foreseen that in 1982 the route would help bring the legacy of Yellowstone full circle. Prior to the eruption of Mount St. Helens, few people realized that the peak fell within the boundaries of the federal land grant awarded in 1864 to the Northern Pacific Railroad to help offset the cost of its construction. Similarly, hardly anyone noticed in 1970 when the remainder of this grant, due to the merger of the Northern Pacific, Great Northern, and Chicago, Burlington, and

The eruption of Mount St. Helens blew 1,313 feet off the top of the 9,677-foot peak. By Lyn Topinka, courtesy of the U.S. Geological Survey.

Quincy railroads, became the property of the restructured corporation, Burlington Northern Inc.

Like any cataclysmic event, the eruption of Mount St. Helens reawakened everyone's interest in these and other details. Burlington Northern in particular was first to sense the new possibilities of America's "pragmatic alliance," the historic spirit of cooperation between business leaders and preservationists that led to the establishment of the national parks.

Richard M. Bressler, chairman and chief executive officer of Burlington Northern Inc., informed President Ronald Reagan of the company's gift on May 17, 1982. "It is our hope," Bressler concluded

Swelling from below, the giant lava dome in the crater of Mount St. Helens is dramatic proof that the peak will eventually rebuild itself. By Lyn Topinka, courtesy of the U.S. Geological Survey.

his letter, "that this donation will encourage the careful management of the Mount St. Helens area for the contemplation and enjoyment of future generations."

On May 18, 1983, the third anniversary of the eruption, officials of the United States Forest Service, Burlington Northern Inc., environmental groups, and other interested parties convened for the dedication of the Mount St. Helens National Volcanic Monument and visitor center. Richard Bressler presented a plaque to commemorate the dedication, and further outlined Burlington Northern's historical commitment to scenic preservation. Although the boundaries of the monument had not been laid out to the satisfaction of everyone concerned, no one disagreed that the protection of Mount St. Helens symbolized another positive moment in American conservation.

And so, thanks to that eventful May 18 three years earlier, Burlington Northern Inc., added another chapter to the history of railroad philanthropy on behalf of the American land. Mount St. Helens offered another geography of hope. Indeed, not since the discovery of the original national parks of the American West had any landmark so captivated the American imagination, so reaffirmed the nation's pride in its breathtaking natural beauty.

SIX ⊗

RETURN TO
GRAND CANYON

*When I first heard of the Santa Fe trains running to the edge of the Grand Cañon of
Arizona, I was troubled with thoughts of the disenchantment likely to follow. But last winter, when I saw those trains crawling along through the pines of the Coconino Forest and
close up to the brink of the chasm at Bright Angel, I was glad to discover that in the presence of such stupendous scenery they are nothing. The locomotives and trains are mere bee-
tles and caterpillars, and the noise they make is as little disturbing as the hooting of an owl
in the lonely woods.*

John Muir, *Century Magazine*, November 1902

Almost without exception, Americans judge the value
of any technology foremost in terms of age. Newer is better—indeed
what is new *must* be better—or so most Americans still confidently
believe. Given that standard bias, the revival of the Grand Canyon
Railway on September 17, 1989, seems all the more remarkable. To be
sure, the twenty-year dream to restore the famous branch line ran
counter to the opinions of many acknowledged "experts." The public,
it was commonly argued, preferred automobiles over trains. Few people
would ride a train to the Grand Canyon if they could still drive their
cars. The passenger train, to put it bluntly, was too slow and old-
fashioned. The future of transportation everywhere was still in highways and modern airports.

Historically, that argument crested in the 1960s, as all across the
United States name passenger trains were downgraded, then abandoned. Citing its own loss of riders, in 1968 the Atchison, Topeka &
Santa Fe Railway discontinued passenger service on its historic branch
line between Williams, Arizona, and Grand Canyon National Park.
Effectively abandoned, the route was now seriously in danger of being
scrapped. Nonetheless, a few people kept alive the possibility of restoring it as an alternative for visitor access, among them historians and

The Santa Fe Railway's first train to the South Rim of the Grand Canyon, September 17, 1901, was cause for celebration and this official photograph. Courtesy of the Santa Fe Railway Company.

environmentalists concerned about escalating development along the canyon's South Rim.

Constantly strapped for capital, however, such proposals kept getting nowhere. Well into the 1980s it appeared the railroad would still be lost. Suddenly (some would say miraculously) the problem of funding was overcome. In 1987, investors from Phoenix, Max and Thelma Biegert, bought out the railroad, incorporating it as the Grand Canyon Railway. Moving swiftly to restore it, in January 1989 they announced the resumption of rail passenger service by April 1990. Then came a wonderful change of plans—the opening had been pushed *forward* eight months. As reannounced, it would be September 17, 1989, exactly eighty-eight years since the first Santa Fe passenger train had called at South Rim.

Working around the clock, construction crews rushed to meet the deadline, rehabilitating all sixty-five miles of track and a historic steam locomotive. So, too, the combination Harvey House and depot in

A mile deep, miles wide, & painted like a sunset

That's the <u>Grand Canyon</u> of Arizona

For art booklets of the train and trip address
W. J. Black. Pass. Traffic Mgr.
A.T & S.F. Ry. System,
1051 Railway Exchange, Chicago

You can go there in a Pullman to the rim at El Tovar, en route to Sunny California on the train of luxury

The California Limited

Santa Fe
All the way

Does the handsome young ranger have the lady's full attention? If not, how can he blame her for being distracted by something so deep, so wide, and "painted like a sunset?" Advertisement from the December 1910 issue of *McClure's* magazine. Courtesy of the Santa Fe Railway Company.

The first passenger train to Grand Canyon National Park in twenty-one years draws an excited crowd during reinaugural ceremonies at Canyon Depot, September 17, 1989. Photograph by the author.

downtown Williams was meticulously restored, retaining the name Fray Marcos. No less significant, antique passenger coaches were obtained from the Southern Pacific Railroad, then virtually rebuilt, again to reflect the heyday of the Grand Canyon Railway during the 1910s and 1920s.

By the morning of September 17, the air seemed to crackle with the excitement and anticipation. After so many false starts—after so many dashed hopes—a train was actually to depart Williams for Grand Canyon National Park. Beneath swirling clouds and intermittent showers, two thousand people pressed forward to hear what the dignitaries had to say. Most agreed the railroad would be instrumental in eliminating automobiles from Grand Canyon National Park. Otherwise, the pinnacle of the ceremony was a subtle bow to history. In tribute to the reinaugural, the artist Fred Lucas presented the people of Arizona with a large painting of Grand Canyon to hang in the Capitol. No gift could have been more appropriate for recalling a century of railroad sponsorship on behalf of the national parks. From

Earlier on September 17, during reinaugural ceremonies in Williams, Arizona, artist Fred Lucas commemorated the restoration of the Grand Canyon Railway by presenting the state with a magnificent new painting. Photograph by the author.

Thomas Moran to Fred Lucas, artists had served a pledge within a dream, instilling the conviction that the national parks could be opened both elegantly and responsibly.

The ceremonies completed, the locomotive was finally coupled to the long string of waiting cars. Six hundred people, guests of the Biegerts, had been invited to take the train. Thousands more lined the tracks to watch it heading north out of Williams; another four thousand waited expectantly at Canyon Depot and El Tovar. Predictably, the train's arrival called for another round of speeches and ceremoniously driving a golden spike. A final promise was no less significant — historic Canyon Depot would also be restored.

Returning to Williams, the train seemed mystically to carry its riders back to a simpler, less hurried age. A benediction of clearing skies and glowing twilight further confirmed that it had been an amazing day. A historic railroad had been reborn instead of thoughtlessly abandoned. An opportunity for saving Grand Canyon from the automobile finally seemed both prudent and attainable.

Today averaging 130,000 riders, the historic route annually displaces more than fifty thousand cars. Confident that visitors would do even more, over the years the railroad has proposed that motor vehicles be eliminated altogether. It would further establish a light-rail system based in Tusayan, Grand Canyon's most popular gateway. At Tusayan, all day-use visitors would exit their cars and buses for entry via rail, with principal stops at Mather Point and the periphery of the historic district. Ideally, extensions east and west of Canyon Village would also be operational in ten to fifteen years.

Symbolic of 1901, the restoration of 1989 recalls the historic age of railroad travel in the West. No less expectantly than their forebears, visitors may depart Williams for Grand Canyon behind classic steam and diesel locomotives. The system of light-rail looks to the future, acknowledging the need to plan for Grand Canyon National Park beyond the usual conservative, halting increments.

With visitation expected to double or triple within twenty to thirty years, cars and buses are not the answer. Only railroads have the capacity to carry those additional visitors without intruding on the landscape. Aboard the Grand Canyon Railway, a million riders have already rediscovered that timeless promise of a train. Beginning September 17, 1989, Americans repeated a piece of their history, and found that old can indeed be as good as new.

Top. The Grand Canyon Looking West from Mojave Point (1929), by Gunnar Widforss. Courtesy of the Burlington Northern Santa Fe Collection of Southwestern Art. *Above.* The restored Grand Canyon Railway offers many colorful sights and sounds reminiscent of the Old West. Photograph by Al Richmond, courtesy of the Grand Canyon Railway.

To this day, the North Rim of the Grand Canyon, historically served by the Union Pacific Railroad, is the wilder and less accessible side. Indeed, little of the North Rim's flavor has changed since the Union Pacific commissioned this colorful advertisement for publication in May 1927. Signed H. Foster. Shown approximate original size. Author's collection.

In May 1993, Princess Tours introduced its third Ultra Dome to the *Midnight Sun Express* (top), providing luxury service bertween Anchorage and Fairbanks, Alaska, via Denali National Park. Rail enthusiasts are hopeful that comparable visibility will one day be restored to Amtrak's western trains, such as the *Coast Starlight*, which parallels the Pacific Ocean for 110 miles between Oxnard and Surf, California. Above: The *Starlight* is shown crossing Gaviota Trestle at Gaviota Beach State Park, northwest of Santa Barbara, in January 1977. Dome interior courtesy of Princess Tours. *Starlight* photograph by the author.

Glacier Morning, by J. Craig Thorpe. High above the Middle Fork of the Flathead River bordering Glacier National Park, Montana, Amtrak's eastbound *Empire Builder* affords a panoramic view of Goat Lick and a tumble of forested mountainsides. Oil on canvas, 18 by 14 inches. Copyright 1996 by J. Craig Thorpe. From the private collection of Dr. and Mrs. A. Louis Steplock, Jr. Courtesy of the artist.

SEVEN ⊗
DISCOVERY TODAY

Americans have tragically deserted the most heroic dimension of their own continent: size. With many other Europeans, I feel that Americans are strangers to their own country in a way that no European can be. One reason is the demise of the American railroad.

Clive Irving, *Condé Nast Traveler*, September 1992

The distinction between traveling for business or for pleasure is what sets travel itself apart, and why—at least in the United States—we have so few trains left to choose from. In America, every emphasis is still on speed. The following sample of classic park itineraries is for those who still insist that travel should be an adventure, not another mirror image of what is ordinary or everyday. These pages, then, are for those who accept rail transportation not only as the best hope for saving the national parks, but also for preserving travel itself as something grand and unforgettable.

GLACIER NATIONAL PARK

Gateway Train: **Empire Builder** (Amtrak) toll-free in the U.S. 1-800-USA-RAIL (1-800-872-7245).

Service Frequency: Daily (subject to change).

Arrival: The *Empire Builder* makes three stops: East Glacier Park Station (Glacier Park Lodge), Essex (Izaak Walton Inn), and West Glacier (Lake McDonald Lodge). As necessary, shuttles meet the train and carry passengers to their hotels. Off-season, the *Empire Builder* bypasses East Glacier Park Station and stops at Browning, fourteen miles farther east.

Principal Departure Cities: Chicago–Seattle/Portland. Westbound, train splits at Spokane, Washington, operating as a northern section to

Seattle and a southern section to Portland, Oregon. Eastbound, train separately departs Portland and Seattle, rejoining in Spokane. Continuing full-train service eastbound to Glacier, Fargo, Minneapolis–Saint Paul, Milwaukee, and Chicago. Connections at Chicago (Union Station) for all eastern points.

The Roof of the Continent

If there is such a thing as time travel, then the *Empire Builder* to Glacier National Park is the quintessential time machine. The moment the doors swing open the train seems to lose a century, as if it were 1920 all over again. The mood is especially pronounced at East Glacier Park station, as if, suffused within the walls, it springs forth to enchant arriving passengers. More imposing still, Glacier Park Lodge rises directly opposite, enveloping the crest of a long, gentle incline. Passengers take a pathway lined with flower beds and enter the cavernous building, where the atmosphere yet again seems almost mystical and subdued. Cathedral-like, giant logs five hundred years old rib the entire lobby, accented with original paintings and mementos from the days of the Great Northern Railway.

Granted, other parks have railroad structures, yet none is a threshold as grand as this. Added to luxury it proclaims accessibility, the only flagship national park that was ever located on a railroad's main line. Indeed, no other track is more distinctive, and by serendipity so heartwarmingly anachronistic. Glacier retains not only its blissful isolation but also the singular convenience of its history. The park may be equally dependent on highways, true, but visitors also flock west aboard the train, enticed by the knowledge that the railroad is indeed a wondrous link with Glacier's past.

Rising to frame the hotel, the mountains also seem to call out for an artist, as if no postcard or common photograph could ever validate their contribution to the scene. It is another ambiance made doubly suggestive by the proximity of the train. Not only its presence, but again its continuity, best explain why Glacier never lost the feelings of an original railroad park. Ever deeper into the heart of the wilderness, paralleling the park for more than fifty miles, only the *Empire Builder* has brooked no rivals for marking both the flow of time and history.

The grandeur of Canada is further acknowledged; indeed, Glacier is actually two parks in one. Established in 1895, Waterton Lakes National Park, Alberta, adjoins at the U.S.–Canadian border, which the parks share for approximately twenty miles. Designated Waterton/Glacier International Peace Park in 1932, both units have been separately managed, although consistently in recognition of their common boundary and shared wildlife populations.

For soaking up the historical ambiance, nothing beats staying over in one or more of Glacier's famed hotels, that is, those originally constructed under the auspices of the Great Northern Railway. Besides Glacier Park Lodge (1913), there is Many Glacier Hotel (1915) on Swiftcurrent Lake, and the stunning Prince of Wales Hotel (1927) at Waterton Lakes, Canada. Built separately in 1914, Lake McDonald Lodge joined the railroad's holdings in 1930, when Great Northern purchased and renovated the property. "The original building," the railway nonetheless reassured patrons, "still provides accommodations of rustic charm and beauty."

Winter Tracks, by J. Craig Thorpe. Open year round, Glacier's Izaak Walton Inn offers a setting unmatched for discovering nature or simply enjoying trains, such as the *Empire Builder* arriving daily from Chicago and Seattle. Oil on canvas, 14 by 18 inches. Copyright 1996 by J. Craig Thorpe. From the private collection of Dr. and Mrs. A. Louis Steplock, Jr. Courtesy of the artist.

The perfect complement to the *Empire Builder* and the historic hotels is the fleet of motor stages operated by Glacier Park, Inc. Instantly recognized in their dazzling livery (bright red with jet black fenders), classic originals date from 1936. Hope for sunshine, a nip in the air, and Glacier's brilliant blue skies, all signaling your driver to break out the woolen blankets and roll back the canvas covering.

The top either up or down, nothing compares with the breathtaking views along the Going-to-the-Sun Road. Heading west to east, the road parallels Lake McDonald and rushing McDonald Creek, ascends the Garden Wall, crosses windswept Logan Pass (elevation 6,649 feet), and drops again to the shores of majestic St. Mary Lake, all within barely fifty miles.

At Essex, the Izaak Walton Inn is another nostalgic park experience, and the only major hotel to provide accommodations and serious activities throughout the year. Your shuttle awaits as you disembark from the *Empire Builder*, which stops just a quarter mile away. In summer, a full complement of activities includes white-water rafting, guided hikes, and all-day tours; in winter, miles of groomed trails lure cross-country skiers from Canada, Europe, and the United States.

Even then, it is the hotel many come to see, with its picture windows facing the tracks and its historic railroad ambiance, beautifully recalled in paintings, photographs, and other classic memorabilia from the Great Northern Railway. Constructed by the railroad in 1939, it served originally as a dormitory, housing workers isolated in the Rocky Mountains by the long distances and winter snows. The porch and dining room are wonderful for watching trains, especially when helper engines emerge from the adjacent siding to assist heavy freights headed east over Marias Pass. Obviously, the Rocky Mountains are still capable of thwarting national commerce, if not the inn's increasing stream of contented guests. Most find, amid the scenery and the isolation, no finer spot for thrilling to the best of nature or the wistful interruptions of mountain trains.

For More Information

Glacier National Park: Write the Superintendent, Glacier National Park, West Glacier, Montana 59936. Or call: (406) 888-7800.

Cooperating Association (guidebooks, trail guides, seminars, and other specialized information): Write the Glacier Natural History Association, P. O. Box 428, West Glacier, Montana 59936. Or call: (406) 888-5756.

Park Lodging and Guided Tours: Call Glacier Park, Inc., at (602) 207-6000. From Canada the number is (403) 236-3400. Or write: Glacier Park, Inc., East Glacier, Montana 59434-0147, or Viad Tower, Phoenix, Arizona 85077-0928.

Izaak Walton Inn: Write: P. O. Box 653, Essex, Montana 59916. Or phone: (406) 888-5700.

GRAND CANYON NATIONAL PARK

Gateway Train: **Williams Flyer** (Grand Canyon Railway) toll-free in the U.S. 1-800-THE-TRAIN (1-800-843-8724).

Closest Amtrak Service: **Southwest Chief** (via Flagstaff) toll-free in the U.S. 1-800-USA-RAIL. (1-800-872-7245). SPECIAL NOTE: A direct transfer to the Grand Canyon Railway at Williams is under consideration. Check with Amtrak, the Grand Canyon Railway, or your travel agent.

Service Frequencies: Grand Canyon Railway, daily except Christmas Eve and Christmas Day; Amtrak, daily (subject to change).

Arrival: The *Williams Flyer* makes one stop in Grand Canyon National Park, at the historic Canyon Depot (El Tovar Hotel; Bright Angel Lodge; Maswik Lodge; Yavapai Lodge). Current Amtrak connections via Flagstaff are by bus.

Principal Departure Cities: The *Williams Flyer* departs Williams, 31 miles west of Flagstaff and 65 miles south of Canyon Village in Grand Canyon National Park. Amtrak's *Southwest Chief* departs Los Angeles (eastbound) and Chicago (westbound), including intermediate stops at Kansas City, Lamy (Santa Fe), and Albuquerque.

The Titan of Chasms

Set unobtrusively below the rim, Canyon Depot gives no hint of the majesty that has long awaited your arrival. You are directed to take the steps behind the depot, then continue to the stone wall straight ahead. However brief, no walk in North America is more distinctive or significant. After all, millions have preceded you, similarly ascending between Grand Canyon Railway and the brink of geological time.

Indeed, visitors have gathered here for at least a century, further escorted between history and natural history by the rustic elegance of El Tovar. Implicitly, the building salutes arriving guests, facing south across the tracks and Canyon Depot. Opposite it overlooks the upper layers of the canyon, the North Rim colorfully pinpointed by a distant crown of green. Although Grand Canyon needs no architectural embellishments, the hotel definitely contributed to its popularity and preservation. Thanks to the Santa Fe Railway, by 1919 the "titan of chasms" had attracted enough visitors to justify its establishment as one of America's flagship national parks.

Granted, automobiles have predominated since 1930, but all of the romance and the best scenery are still experienced aboard the train. The highway runs several miles to the east, touching the railroad very briefly north of Williams. The railroad otherwise keeps its distance, as

Its cover featuring El Tovar, this lovely brochure by the Atchison, Topeka & Santa Fe Railway (1915) describes scenes along Hermit Rim Road, now West Rim Drive. Note Grand Canyon's original form of public transportation. Brochure 5¾ by 8½ inches. Author's collection.

if resolute about escaping any roads and their likely pockmarks of development. Loyally following its historical route, the track crests the plateau and several banks of rolling hills, offering kaleidoscopic views of the San Francisco Mountains. If blessed by summer rains, wildflowers also push brilliantly between the ties, gently bent but rarely pruned by the trains gliding overhead.

Like the bottom of a wide bowl, the plateau is deepest at its center. The South Rim of Grand Canyon dramatically awaits, but only after the railroad has restored 1,500 feet of elevation. It is a wondrous, exciting climb, the train twisting into the deepening forest while veering past hanging branches and yellow cliffs. Even now, still far back from the highway, there is little suggestive of civilization to break the spell. If expectation requires isolation, indeed, the highway is not even a tad adventurous. Rather, it is the railroad still keeping faith with the spirit of discovery first extolled by canyon visitors.

The arrival at Canyon Depot similarly recalls the difference between historical grandeur and a tourist trap. One moment the train is wedged between stately pines; the next El Tovar breaks regally into view, crowning the bluff above the station. Other nearby landmarks, among them Hopi House and Bright Angel Lodge, are added reminders that the railroad brought architectural taste along with appropriate transportation.

In any institution, whatever promotes responsibility is likely to be especially cherished and enduring. Long a focus of public transit, Grand Canyon National Park inspires visitors to consider options other than always relying on the automobile. Most notably, alone among the original parks it is closest to being served by a modern system of light-rail, as consistently advocated by the Grand Canyon Railway and formally proposed in 1996. On November 25, 1997, Interior Secretary Bruce Babbitt officially announced light-rail as the government's own preferred alternative.

Meanwhile, cars are still purposely discouraged as a burden on the solitude and the scenery. In summer, shuttles ply between Canyon Village and Hermits Rest along the spectacular West Rim Drive. Off-season, a generous complement of sponsored tours still take full advantage of the route. Hikers may have it best. The scenic Rim Trail is conveniently accessible from everywhere in Canyon Village; likewise, Bright Angel Trail is just moments from several lodges and the steps of El Tovar.

The uniqueness of Grand Canyon lies in that enduring celebration of both earth and human time. In its depths, rocks perhaps two billion

years old predate the dawn of life itself. Along the rim, cultural
resources such as El Tovar may commemorate only the past century of
modern history, yet in terms of preservation no period has counted
more. As soon as Grand Canyon was served by train, preservationists
enlisted the railroad as their most important ally. Even Grand Canyon
was no match for civilization unless its natural forces could be celebrated, then secured. Such was the promise of the railroad, arriving
September 17, 1901. Surely it is a promise still worth keeping, as
undoubtedly your own adventures aboard the Grand Canyon Railway
will also move you to reattest.

No Traffic, by J. Craig Thorpe. If opened to light-rail, the heart of the historic district in
Canyon Village, Grand Canyon National Park, likely would appear much as it did in the early
1900s, absent horse-drawn carriages and the congestion of today's motor vehicles. In this
artist's conception, light-rail coaches in the foreground adapt easily into the existing roadway
while, just beyond, visitors disembark from the vintage train, restored in 1989. Although not
included in the historic district, a comparable light-rail system won government approval in
November 1997. Oil on canvas, 20 by 24 inches. Copyright 1997 by J. Craig Thorpe.
Collection of the Grand Canyon Railway. Courtesy of the artist.

For More Information

Grand Canyon National Park: Write Superintendent, Grand Canyon National Park, P. O. Box 129, Grand Canyon, Arizona 86023. Or call: (520) 638-7888.

Cooperating Association (guidebooks, trail guides, seminars, and other specialized information): Write the Grand Canyon Association, P. O. Box 399, Grand Canyon, Arizona 86023. Or call: (520) 638-2481.

Park Lodging and Guided Tours, South Rim (Fred Harvey Inc.): Write Grand Canyon National Park Lodges, Grand Canyon, Arizona 86023. Or call: (303) 297-2757.

Train and Lodging Packages, Williams or South Rim: Call 1-800-THE-TRAIN. Or write Fray Marcos Hotel, Grand Canyon Railway, 235 North Grand Canyon Boulevard, Williams, Arizona 86046.

DENALI NATIONAL PARK AND PRESERVE

Gateway Train(s): **Denali Star** (Alaska Railroad) 1-800-544-0552; **McKinley Explorer** (Holland America Westours–Gray Line of Alaska) 1-800-544-2206; **Midnight Sun Express** (Princess Tours) 1-800-835-8907.

Service Frequency: Full trains operate daily in season, approximately mid-May to mid-September. Call the Alaska Railroad (1-800-544-0552) for schedules, equipment, and frequencies of operation the remainder of the year.

Arrival: Denali (Mount McKinley) National Park and Preserve is the inspiration for and principal destination of this train. Arrival is noon (southbound from Fairbanks) and mid afternoon (northbound from Anchorage). Package tours and special itineraries provide for any necessary layovers and accommodations. With few exceptions, the park is off-limits to private cars; regular entry is by bus.

Principal Departure Cities: Trains depart Anchorage and Fairbanks as a single unit operated by the Alaska Railroad. Forward are the engines and *Denali Star* of the Alaska Railroad; the middle train set is the *McKinley Explorer*; the final set is the *Midnight Sun Express*.

The Last Frontier

The moment I saw the great train standing in the station, I felt a rush of emotions I had not recalled in many years. It was early fall in Anchorage, Alaska, where I had come to ride the *McKinley Explorer* north to Denali National Park. I immediately recognized the train's classic exterior like the face of a long-lost friend, reminiscent of the great western streamliners I had grown up with in the 1950s. The western railroads—and several in the East—had reequipped their passenger fleets with brand new vista-domes. Some, like those of the *McKinley Explorer*, stretched the length of the entire car, materially adding to the number of passengers who could enjoy the incredible views.

Now, on the Last Frontier, I hoped to relive that Golden Age. In that case, the *McKinley Explorer* would have to be more than a facade, playacting the past without substance and sincerity. Rather, it would suggest a part of life—something seamless, something real, and not just a "marketed" reenactment.

Barely minutes out of Anchorage my doubts had already been put to rest. The *McKinley Explorer* was immersed in authenticity, enveloped by a landscape breathtaking in its ability to encapsulate the natural history of North America. Mountains rose on either horizon, their flanks brilliant in autumn yellow. A moose bounded beside the train, then ducked off into the nearby underbrush. Mile after mile the train slipped deeper into the vast, encircling wilderness, finally rising above the endless forest to climb into the imposing Alaska Range.

Definitely, this was not some oval in an amusement park or a steam ride through suburbia. Rather, I felt transported back to the American West of a century ago—only the railroad to suggest change, and that but a ribbon laid beside the thundering rivers or dropped over their narrow canyons. This was railroading as I longed to recall it, a celebration rather than a confrontation between a landscape and a technology. I was on a real train, going somewhere I had never been, through a landscape resplendent with natural beauty and ringing with names I had never heard of.

Alaska Range, by J. Craig Thorpe. In a rare tribute to the timeless qualities of traditional railroad art, in 1994 the Alaska Railroad and Holland America Westours commissioned this painting of their combined trains approaching Denali National Park and Preserve. Oil on canvas, 24 by 18 inches. Copyright 1994 by J. Craig Thorpe. Courtesy of the artist.

It still had to be the train, I concluded. Designed and built by the Budd Company, the cars of the *McKinley Explorer* initially operated on the Santa Fe Railway, showcasing the desert Southwest. True, Budd may have exaggerated just a bit by claiming their stainless-steel construction would last as long as the pyramids. Then again, although it had not been four thousand years it had certainly been forty-five, time enough for any piece of equipment to have been retired, and probably scrapped.

Beautifully restored, the cars instead survived, now to glide effortlessly—elegantly—across the face of Alaska. "It's the six-wheel trucks," one attendant carefully explained. "And the lower center of gravity," another added. Pride of construction—intended for a life-time—ultimately explains why each car is so stable, so elegant, and of exceptional durability.

Two other trains bracket the *McKinley Explorer*, each distinctive in its own right. The diesel engines and first train set, the *Denali Star*, are owned by the Alaska Railroad. Vintage cars mix comfortably with newer equipment, each featuring, to the delight of riders, a taste of Alaska as it was. Immediately behind come the full-length vista domes of the *McKinley Explorer*, four to six cars in all. The third train set, the *Midnight Sun Express*, also features full-length domes, known in the industry as ultra domes. Obviously, there is a competitive spirit among all three operators, but also a genuine sense of accomplishment and cooperation. After all, through their combined efforts the train has evolved to become the longest—and among the most elegant—of its kind anywhere in the United States.

A glimpse of Mount McKinley was all I needed to round out a perfect day. True, I planned to enter the park the following morning, trekking by bus 190 miles round trip on the dirt road to Wonder Lake. A distant landmark, however, always excites the romance of the journey in between. Suddenly, there it was—Mount McKinley—grandly inviting a closer inspection of its enormous flanks and sprawling glaciers. Pulling into Denali station, I imagined myself a century earlier at Gardiner, Montana, making the transfer across the platform into a stagecoach bound for Yellowstone. It must have been just like this—the train, the hubbub, and the anticipation of the grandeur yet to come. The next day, I would be one of only twenty-five thousand people annually making the pilgrimage all the way to Wonder Lake. Like historic Yellowstone, I thought again, except that my stagecoach tomorrow morning would be running on diesel or gasoline.

"Outside," as Alaskans call it, wilderness of such proportions—of such sweeping magnificence—is largely a distant memory. It awaits you in Denali, however, and all along the Alaska Railroad. Alaska means stepping back to when the country everywhere was fresh and young. Aboard the *McKinley Explorer*, I felt the vibrancy of the present blending effortlessly with that quality of the past. Yet again, a train had proved that the going there, not just the getting there, is what life and travel are all about.

For More Information

Denali National Park: Write Superintendent, Denali National Park and Preserve, P. O. Box 9, Denali Park, Alaska 99755. Or call (907) 683-2294.

Cooperating Association (guidebooks, trail guides, seminars, and other specialized information): Write the Alaska Natural History Association, P. O. Box 230, Denali Park, Alaska 99755. Or call (907) 683-1272.

Park Lodging and Guided Tours: The principal railroad companies operate their own lodges or cooperative facilities just outside the park. Contact Holland America Westours, Princess Tours, and the Alaska Railroad at the numbers listed above. The official park concessionaire is Denali Park Resorts, 241 West Ship Creek Avenue, Anchorage, Alaska 99501. Call 1-800-276-7234.

In the Heart of the Park: The classic wilderness experience is Camp Denali, including nearby North Face Lodge. Write Camp Denali, P. O. Box 67, Denali Park, Alaska 99755. Or call (907) 683-2290.

THE NATIONAL PARKS UNLIMITED

Gateway Train: **American Orient Express** (American Orient Express Railway Company) toll-free in the U. S. 1-888-759-3944. Or write American Orient Express Railway Company, 1660 Wynkoop, Suite 1160, Denver, Colorado 80202.

Service Frequency: Varies seasonally by route and program, April through October. Call for complimentary brochures and departure schedules.

Principal Departure Cities: Santa Fe, Denver, Los Angles, Portland, and Seattle.

Principal National Parks Visited: Yellowstone, Grand Teton, Glacier, Grand Canyon, Zion, Bryce, Jasper (Alberta, Canada).

A Window on the West

The idea that a train could be a national park is perhaps long overdue. Although a number of museums and historical sites commemorate the

A great new train —THE CALIFORNIA ZEPHYR

Three railroads—the Burlington, the Denver & Rio Grande Western, and the Western Pacific—are placing in operation on March 20th six all-stainless steel trains built by Budd, to provide a new daily service between Chicago and San Francisco over a scenic route of incomparable grandeur.

These are the spectacular new California Zephyrs—trains of almost unbelievable beauty and luxury. Their Vista-Domes, de-luxe coaches, cars reserved for women and children, lounges, diners and most modern of all transcontinental sleepers offer travel enjoyment beyond your dreams.

The California Zephyrs traverse some of the finest scenery in the world, and their schedules, in both directions, permit you to enjoy the most exciting portions during daylight hours ... the serried peaks of the highest Colorado Rockies ... Gore and Glenwood Canyons ... snowy Sierras ... and California's fabulous Feather River Canyon of gold rush fame.

Another incentive to travel on these wonderful trains is the fact that they are constructed, not merely sheathed, with stainless steel, the strongest material used in building railway cars. Beneath their gleaming surface these cars have structures of the same lustrous metal, three times as strong as ordinary steel. In the United States, the only all-stainless steel cars are built by Budd ... and Budd builds no other kind. The Budd Company, Philadelphia 32, Pa.

Periodically reprising the spectacular route of the *California Zephyr,* shown here in the advertising art of Leslie Ragan, the *American Orient Express* pierces the Rocky Mountains west of Denver through the canyons of the Colorado River. Courtesy of the Budd Company.

origins of railroad technology, rarely are they associated with movement on a scale commensurate with the history. Trains are indeed about movement, the bridging of countries and entire continents. Recapturing the importance of American railroading requires a sense of passage, not just a lifeless, fixed exhibit. The experiences previously described above fall elegantly into that category, providing, through the gift of motion, authentic expectation and a spirit of true adventure. Unlike a museum, each train features not only a fixed point of origin but also the distances it historically covered, and overcame.

And so it remains with the *American Orient Express*, undoubtedly America's most elegant park on rails. If the object is to save not only the technology, but more, the sensations it once aroused, then to step aboard the *American Orient Express* is to experience those sensations on the grandest scale imaginable. Each of its fifteen cars is vintage, all from the 1940s and 1950s. Meticulously restored, they reflect the heyday of America's Pullman trains, when luxury was the operable word and elegance meant sparing no expense.

Yet, it is more than the mahogany paneling, spacious lounges, and fine dining that set the *American Orient Express* apart. It is still the train's ability to recall the past without resorting to fakery or theatrics. Mention a great train of the West and the *American Orient Express* probably traces major portions of the same route today, traces it, that is, as if more than mimicking a sense of history. In the Colorado Rockies, for example, it follows in the footsteps of the renowned *California Zephyr*, whose vista domes revolutionized passenger railroading beginning in 1949. "We go through the Rockies, not around them," proclaimed the Denver & Rio Grande Western Railroad. And so the *California Zephyr* did, piercing the Front Range out of Denver through the brooding darkness of Moffat Tunnel, then bursting into sunlight to follow the Colorado River west through a series of massive, twisted canyons.

Deceptively, at first, the mountains appear to be impenetrable. Suddenly, the barrier is rapidly giving way, even the horizon lost in a cavernous hollow rent between steep, imposing cliffs. Our locomotives have already committed us; momentarily, we follow them bravely in, coursing headlong beside the Colorado River past boiling rapids and jagged rocks. Finally, the water calms and slackens, as if also pausing to gather courage for the next canyon just beyond. Time and again the process repeats, until at last the Rockies loom behind us rather than above the rooftops of our train.

Days later, in northern New Mexico, the Colorado Rockies are only a distant memory. Enveloped now by mesas, we streak for Arizona along the route of the fabled Atchison, Topeka & Santa Fe. No less faithful to that railroad's colorful history, the *American Orient Express* will enter Grand Canyon National Park over the restored Grand Canyon Railway.

Ready to depart Grand Canyon National Park over the restored Grand Canyon Railway, the *American Orient Express* recalls every commitment to luxury and glamour generally ascribed only to America's classic, vanished trains. Photograph by the author.

Returning to the Williams depot, our train will be spotlessly cleaned and serviced. Then it is back to the main line, enjoying a sunset, and perhaps a rainbow, during our evening departure for California.

At Barstow we change course, now following the tracks of the Union Pacific northeast across the uplift of the great Mojave Desert. In Utah passengers disembark for tours of Zion and Bryce Canyon national parks. It is all deep canyons here, interspersed with sprawling desert. It is the West as it used to be, and which, apart from the glitter of Las Vegas, largely still survives, resplendent in its isolation and that sense of mystery only true remoteness can arouse.

A railroad museum is a wonderful thing, but is not the reality far superior to its memorial? Merely the thought of a museum implies the end, what is no longer useful but rather dead. Railroading is hardly dead, merely our appreciation of its durability and significance. Trains are not about to be pushed off the continent, even if those still welcoming passengers are so much fewer and far between.

It is a matter of insisting that technology not overrun the national landscape. Should transportation help improve the country, or rather tear endlessly into what remains of its diversity? There is great beauty in the national parks, but ultimately even they are little better than reservations. More is required to ensure that other landscapes are not overwhelmed simply because they are still outside the gates. If Americans hope to preserve where they live, not just where they vacation, it will take a consistency of commitment through appropriate technology. It will take trains like the *American Orient Express*, inventiveness committed to the belief that technology and natural beauty can still somehow abide as one.

FINAL TIPS

Keep abreast of new services and changing itineraries through a knowledgeable travel partner. The following have worldwide reputations, equally for their emphasis on rail travel and on guided tours of the national parks:

National Parks and Conservation Association (NPCA): Call NPCA Travel Program at 1-800-NAT-PARK (1-800-628-7275), ext. 136. Or write NPCA at 1776 Massachusetts Avenue, N.W., Washington, D.C. 20036.

PVA Travel Planning: Call 1-800-795-5700. Or write Peter Voll Associates, 2600 El Camino Real, Suite 609, Palo Alto, California 94306-1705.

Rail Travel Center: Call 1-800-458-5394. Or write Rail Travel Center, 139 Main Street, Suite 606 B, Brattleboro, Vermont 05301.

The National Park Service maintains two sites of exceptional interest in the development of the modern American Railroad:

Golden Spike National Historic Site, P. O. Box 897, Brigham City, Utah 84302. Phone (801) 471-2209. Replica locomotives (the *Jupiter* and 119) reenact the Great Event, the completion of the first transcontinental railroad on May 10, 1869.

Steamtown National Historic Site, 150 South Washington Avenue, Scranton, Pennsylvania 18503. Phone (717) 340-5200. Features museum, restored roundhouse, and former shops of the Delaware, Lackawanna & Western Railroad. Lengthy steam-powered excursions, using heavy, main line locomotives, further enliven the interpretation of railroading in the first half of the twentieth century.

... *In all its Glory*

Here—you are riding in the dome of one of the planetarium cars of the Missouri Pacific Railroad's Colorado Eagle.

The mighty Rockies fairly leap from the Colorado plain. Sunrise sets their towering peaks on fire. What a pity to confine this wild majesty to the capsule of a window frame! From the dome you look ahead . . . above . . . behind. The whole scene is yours in all its glory.

Five of the nation's great railroads will have dome cars this year. They are the world's finest cars, built by Budd, originator of the stainless steel streamliner, and sole builder of all-stainless steel railroad cars—the strongest and safest ever to glide along a glistening rail. The Budd Company, Philadelphia.

Budd

The conviction that technology might complement the grandeur of unspoiled western landscapes is boldly portrayed in this 1948 advertisement featuring the art of Leslie Ragan, who painted similar scenes for the Budd Company well into the 1950s. The accent is on visibility, on the pleasures of discovering the American West through the picture-window effect of Budd's new vista-domes. From *Holiday* magazine, reprinted with permission of the Budd Company.

EPILOGUE ⊗
THE FUTURE
OF DISCOVERY

No one who is in a hurry is really quite civilized. —Mark Twain (attributed)

*It is hard for me to believe that I shall find fair landscapes or sufficient
wildness and freedom behind the eastern horizon.* —Henry David Thoreau, 1851

Few have discerned the singular importance of the
American West with greater insight than the ecologist, Aldo Leopold.
"I am glad I shall never be young without wild country to be young in,"
he wrote in his 1949 classic, *A Sand County Almanac.* "Of what avail
are forty freedoms without a blank spot on the map?" Even as the railroads had speeded the settlement of the West they, too, had learned to
embrace its magnificent "blank spots," extolling scenery and wilderness as natural resources in their own right. The end result was a for-
tuitous linkage between industry and landscape—a great system of
national parks to preserve the best of the region's open spaces, coupled
with modern trains whose every detail, and special attention to observation, evoked a celebration of the West's limitless horizons. To be
sure, innovations like the vista dome were purposely designed to exalt
western scenery. Once, railroad designers and executives, no less than
poets, artists, historians, and ecologists, had understood intuitively
that the spaciousness of the West somehow fulfilled an important psy-
chological need, a belief that in unspoiled landscapes lay the promise
of starting life anew.

"The future lies that way to me," Henry David Thoreau also admitted, divining his nation's fascination with the West as early as 1851.
"The earth seems more unexhausted and richer on that side." Thus he
also groped for words to describe a seductive inner voice that seemed
to guide his daily walks, nudging him "between west and south-

southwest," away from Concord, Walden Pond, and the environs of nearby Boston "toward some particular wood or meadow or deserted pasture or hill in that direction." The key attraction, again, was a landscape that appeared to be uninhabited, in other words, one awaiting discovery. "Eastward I go only by force," he finally summarized his emotions, "but westward I go free."

Fundamentally, that conviction still explains why so many immigrants, foreign visitors, and U.S. citizens alike still look to the West as the region that epitomizes the American experience. The future of discovery, it follows, remains dependent on protecting the landscapes and cultural diversity of the West—more to the point, on their preservation not simply as amusing facades or entertaining artifacts, but rather as vibrant, contributing elements of a genuine regional identity.

As in the past, confronting those challenges will require a deep sense of national purpose. Above all, the system of public refuges whose origins may be traced to the late nineteenth century will have to be protected for centuries yet to come. Throughout the West, those limitless horizons that continue to beckon the imagination are generally the legacy of deliberate, sustained public stewardship.

Once again, it follows, our obligations to the land also call for considering which forms of technology are appropriate to our ends. Defending the public's growing preference for automobiles over railroads, during the 1960s government and industry leaders saddled the passenger train in particular with a crippling pejorative—"unprofitable." With that simple sleight-of-hand, the nation was exempted from all of the disquieting evidence to the contrary, especially the costs of its overreliance on highways and airports. The question Americans now face has nothing to do with defending one travel industry against another but rather: What forms of transportation are best for moving large numbers of people without jeopardizing their safety or destroying the environment?

As we have seen in the pages of this book, the answers often lie in what we choose to celebrate. Of all forms of technology, the railroad has been the most celebrated. Artists in particular have done more than represent the railroad as a historical fact—rather, they have suggested, and convincingly, that railroads have somehow fulfilled society's larger dreams and expectations, having "evolved," so to speak, alongside their surroundings.

That ability of a railroad to slip into the landscape while further capturing the imagination betrays which form of technology still promises the best of national mobility and environmental stewardship. I know of no artist, for example, who deliberately—passionately—celebrates expressways, shopping malls, billboards, or parking lots. Granted, I am aware of artists who depict airplanes, but few who paint airports, and certainly not with the same emotional attachments earlier reserved for classic railroad stations. After all, what is there to celebrate in a faceless slab of concrete? Which image still pleases the mind's eye while stirring some creative impulse—the thought of a passenger train rounding a curve in the heart of the Rocky Mountains, or one of any airport, two-lane highway, or four-lane interstate? Which has left the biggest scar? In short, which seems to "belong" in the landscape and which stands out against it?

If nothing else, I am proud that *Trains of Discovery* has raised such levels of awareness, reawakening its readers to the technical and environmental superiorities of railroad transportation, all the while challenging the myth of the so-called unprofitable passenger train. In the final analysis, however, we need to consider not only what works for us but also what inspires us. Simply, trains are a wonderful way to travel. It used to be commonly said that "time is money." Suddenly, more and more people are coming to realize that time is really *life*. What's the big hurry? So airplanes are faster, but again, is speed really everything? The chance to sit back, relax, and meet new people, not to mention the simple joys of watching the passing countryside, are no less significant than economics or technological assessment as explanations for the current revival in rail passenger travel.

Let us hope, then, that the trend continues, that our trains, like our public lands, will find more friends and defenders. If we should ever lose the possibility of discovery—of personal renewal—would travel itself have any meaning? Which explains, does it not, the historical roots of environmentalism, the emotions deep within the likes of Henry David Thoreau and Aldo Leopold that led, with wondrous inevitability, to our original national parks and wilderness areas.

With more routes of discovery like the Alaska Railroad, the *Empire Builder*, and the Grand Canyon Railway, the possibility still exists for both access and preservation. Indeed, it only stands to reason why trains and the national parks just naturally go together, and why artists have been drawn to celebrating the western railroads as a complementary aesthetic force. May every traveler to the national parks rediscover those same timeless linkages, and, having done so, be rededicated in mind and spirit to preserving the best of the American land and the best means for its salvation.

It can't write.
It can't read.
It doesn't
have a degree.
It never
went to school.
But after books,
it's one of the best
teachers of American
history.

A Note About the Sources

With the exception of this book and my own articles listed below, information about the western railroads and their role in developing the national park system is still widely scattered. Recent titles on the social and cultural history of railroads, however, point to the growing popularity of the broader subject. Studies acknowledging the significance of railroads in the promotion of regional landscapes would include Carlos A. Schwantes, *Railroad Signatures Across the Pacific Northwest* (Seattle and London: University of Washington Press, 1993), and Brad S. Lomazzi, *Railroad Timetables, Travel Brochures & Posters: A History and Guide for Collectors* (Spencertown, New York: Golden Hill Press, 1995). Similarly, there is renewed interest in the work of Susan Danly and Leo Marx, editors, *The Railroad in American Art: Representations of Technological Change* (Cambridge, Massachusetts: The MIT Press, 1988).

For the national parks in particular, the primary sources remain the annual reports of the superintendents of the individual national parks, published by the Government Printing Office, and Record Group 79 of the National Archives, the records of the National Park Service. The J. Horace McFarland Papers, housed in the William Penn Memorial Museum in Harrisburg, Pennsylvania, also provide insightful glimpses into the attitudes of noted preservationists toward the western railroads in the early twentieth century.

For the role of the Northern Pacific Railroad in promoting the establishment of Yellowstone National Park, there are two works by Aubrey L. Haines: *The Yellowstone Story*, two vols. (Yellowstone National Park: Yellowstone Library and Museum Association in cooperation with Colorado Associated University Press, 1977); and *Yellowstone National Park: Its Exploration and Establishment* (Washington, D.C.: Government Printing Office and National Park Service, 1974). In both titles, but especially in the latter, Haines liberally reprints the correspondence suggesting Yellowstone's importance to Jay Cooke and Company. *Nature's Yellowstone* (Albuquerque: University of New Mexico Press, 1974), by Richard A. Bartlett, and *National Parks: The American Experience* (1979, 1987; third edition, Lincoln and London: University of Nebraska Press, 1997), by Alfred Runte, are other scholarly interpretations of the events of 1869–1872.

Thurman Wilkins, *Thomas Moran: Artist of the Mountains* (Norman: University of Oklahoma Press, 1966) further considers the importance of art in the establishment of Yellowstone National Park, and remains a basic source for Moran's relationship with Jay Cooke and A. B. Nettleton. Joni Kinsey, *Thomas Moran and the Surveying of the American West* (Washington, D.C.: Smithsonian Institution Press, 1992), and Nancy K. Anderson, et al., *Thomas Moran* (Washington, D.C.: National Gallery of Art in association with Yale University Press, 1997), elegantly expand on Moran's life and career, conclusively detailing the significance of his commissions with the Northern Pacific and other western railroads.

A stunning *Wonderland* series of guidebooks, published between 1885 and 1906 by the passenger department of the Northern Pacific Railroad, is instructive not only for its stunning portrayals of the railroad's commitment to Yellowstone, but also for its numerous testimonials from travelers about their impressions of the park. Additional articles in the guidebooks cover such topics as agriculture, mining, cities, hunting, and wildlife conservation. *Frederick Billings: A Life* (New York and Oxford: Oxford University Press, 1991), by Robin W. Winks, credits Billings, as president of the Northern Pacific during its construction across Montana, with insisting that its right-of-way should respect the natural beauty of the Yellowstone River Valley. Similarly, Craig Reese, "The Gardiner Gateway to Yellowstone," *The Mainstreeter* 15 (Spring 1996), focuses on the development of the historic branch line between Livingston and the park. The other side of the railroad's management personality, as reflected in its lopsided exchange of lands needed for the establishment of Mount Rainier National Park, is appropriately summarized in John Ise's *Our National Park Policy: A Critical History* (Baltimore: Johns Hopkins University Press, 1961).

For the spread of national park promotion among the other western railroads, there are privately published guidebooks, pamphlets, and advertisements. Especially important is *Sunset* magazine, initially published beginning in 1898 by the passenger department of the Southern Pacific Railroad. Consequently, early issues reveal the intensity of the railroad's efforts to promote the High Sierra parks of California. Similarly, *The Grand Canyon of Arizona* (Chicago: Atchison, Topeka & Santa Fe Railway, 1902), is a luxurious volume in the tradition of *Wonderland* and *Sunset*, replete with pages of quotations from globetrotters and dignitaries who visited the chasm. As a secondary source, *The Great Southwest of the Fred Harvey Company and the Santa Fe Railway*, by Marta Weigle and Barbara A. Babcock, editors (Phoenix: The Heard Museum, 1996), adds measurably to our understanding of the railroad's promotional efforts. In part, the book builds on T. C. McLuhan's fine, earlier work, *Dream Tracks: The Railroad and the American Indian, 1890–1930* (New York: Harry N. Abrams, Inc., 1985). Although specifically about Indians, there is also much on tourism in general, again focusing on the Southwest, the Santa Fe Railway, and the early promotion of Grand Canyon National Park.

For John Muir's impressions of the Southern Pacific Railroad, there is *John Muir and His Legacy: The American Conservation Movement* (Boston and Toronto: Little, Brown and Company, 1981), by Stephen Fox. A noteworthy article is Richard J. Orsi, "'Wilderness Saint' and 'Robber Baron': The Anomalous Partnership of John Muir and the Southern Pacific Company for Preservation of Yosemite National Park," *Pacific Historian* 29 (Summer/Fall 1985): 136–156. Masterfully and exhaustively, Orsi proves that the Southern Pacific Railroad was instrumental in the establishment of Yosemite and other California parks. Also relevant is Alfred Runte, *Yosemite: The Embattled Wilderness* (Lincoln and London: University of Nebraska Press, 1990). For more on the role of the Milwaukee Road and its subsidiary, the Tacoma Eastern Railroad, there is Arthur D. Martinson, *Wilderness Above the Sound: The Story of Mount Rainier National Park* (Boulder: Roberts Rinehart Publishers, 1994). Similarly, a new history by Thornton Waite, *Yellowstone Branch of the Union Pacific: Route of the Yellowstone Special* (Idaho Falls: Thornton Waite, 1997), beautifully details the efforts of the Union Pacific Railroad to compete for passenger traffic by encouraging travel between Salt Lake City and West Yellowstone via Idaho Falls.

Two publications describe Louis W. Hill and the Great Northern Railway's development of Glacier National Park: Mary Roberts Rinehart, "Through Glacier National Park with Howard Eaton," parts I and II, *Collier's* 57 (April 22 and 29, 1916)[1], and Rufus Steele, "The Son Who Showed His Father: The Story of How Jim Hill's Boy Louis Put a Ladder to the Roof of His Country," *Sunset* 34 (March 1915). The

[1] Currently available in book form as *Through Glacier Park in 1915* (Roberts Rinehart Publishers in cooperation with the Glacier Natural History Association, 1983).

proceedings of the national parks conferences of 1911, 1912, 1915, and 1917, published by the Government Printing Office for the U. S. Department of the Interior, coupled with the hearings on the National Park Service bill before the House Committee on Public Lands, also demonstrate the depth of commitment among the western railroads to the national park system.

For a discussion of the relationship between the railroads and Stephen T. Mather during his tenure as director of the National Park Service, there are two excellent biographies: Robert Shankland, *Steve Mather of the National Parks* (New York: Alfred A. Knopf, 1970), now in its third edition, and Donald C. Swain, *Wilderness Defender: Horace M. Albright and Conservation* (Chicago: University of Chicago Press, 1970). Albright, Mather's assistant and the second director of the National Park Service between 1929 and 1933, donated his personal papers to the University of California, Los Angeles.

A detailed history of the Yosemite Valley Railroad is Hank Johnston, *Railroads of the Yosemite Valley* (Long Beach, California: Johnston-Howe Publications, 1963). The Yosemite National Park Research Library also contains records and photographs of the company.

The emerging interest in railroad advertising as a significant contribution to American art may be found in two special issues of *California History* and *Journal of the West*. In *California History* 70 (Spring 1991), there is my own "Promoting the Golden West: Advertising and the Railroad," pp. 62–75. In *Journal of the West* 31 (January 1992), I add "Promoting Wonderland: Western Railroads and the Evolution of National Park Advertising," pp. 43–48. Kirby Lambert, "The Lure of the Parks," *Montana: The Magazine of Western History* 46 (Spring 1996), skillfully augments my interpretations, including new examples of railroad promotional art, many reproduced in full color.

Turning again to the significance of the trains themselves, especially the ongoing efforts to effect their restoration, the above-mentioned issue of *Journal of the West* contains excellent articles by Al Richmond and Gordon Chappell—Richmond's on the rebuilding of the Grand Canyon Railway, "Renaissance: Breathing New Life into a Legendary Railway," pp. 60–68, and Chappell's on the early development of what was to become Death Valley National Monument, "By Rail to the Rim of Death Valley: Construction of the Death Valley Railroad," pp. 10–19.

Readers will also wish to consult Al Richmond's *Cowboys, Miners, Presidents, and Kings: The Story of the Grand Canyon Railway* (1989), and *Rails to the Rim: Milepost Guide to the Grand Canyon Railway* (1990), both published in Flagstaff, Arizona, by the Grand Canyon Railway. *A Vision for Grand Canyon National Park* (Flagstaff, Arizona: Grand Canyon Railway, 1997), is a stunning, imaginative brochure, employing paintings by J. Craig Thorpe to substantiate Grand Canyon Railway's proposal for a modern, light-rail system. My own "Trains for Parks: A Second Chance," *National Parks* 68 (March/April 1994): 30–34, calls for a similar shift in national thinking from individualism back to community, reasserting that only public transportation can save the national parks from the destructive behavior encouraged by the automobile.

Two books by Joseph Vranich also sharply criticize the nation's foot-dragging in that regard: *Supertrains: Solutions to America's Transportation Gridlock* (New York: St. Martin's Press, 1991), and *Derailed: What Went Wrong and What to Do About America's Passenger Trains* (New York: St. Martin's Press, 1997). Although not about the national parks per se, each has significant observations on the environment and passenger trains as they relate to leisure travel. Undoubtedly, many readers will fault the harsh criticism of Amtrak; nonetheless, Vranich speaks honestly from vast experience and an abiding commitment to the ultimate success of rail passenger service.

Finally, I reaffirm my indebtedness to the National Parks and Conservation Association, and Burlington Northern Inc., for permission to rewrite and republish portions of my work that originally appeared as follows: "Pragmatic Alliance: Western Railroads and the National Parks," *National Parks and Conservation Magazine: The Environmental Journal* 48 (April 1974): 14–21; "Yosemite Valley Railroad: Highway of History, Pathway of Promise," *National Parks and Conservation Magazine: The Environmental Journal* 48 (December 1974): 4–9; and *Burlington Northern and the Dedication of Mount St. Helens: New Legacy of a Proud Tradition* (Seattle: Burlington Northern Inc., 1982).

About the Author

A noted environmental historian, public lecturer, and specialist on the national parks, Alfred Runte lives in Seattle, Washington, where he writes and consults full-time on environmental and transportation issues. Among his other distinguished works are *National Parks: The American Experience* and *Yosemite: The Embattled Wilderness* (both University of Nebraska Press); and *Public Lands, Public Heritage: The National Forest Idea* (also from Roberts Rinehart Publishers). A frequent commentator for the national media, Mr. Runte has contributed to a broad range of national magazines and major newspapers, in addition to television guest appearances on Nightline (ABC), The Today Show (NBC), and Forty-Eight Hours (CBS).